CLUELESS
IN ADVERTISING

CLUELESS
IN ADVERTISING

MAY LWIN
JIM AITCHISON

Prentice
Hall

Singapore   London   New York   Toronto   Sydney   Tokyo   Madrid
Mexico City   Munich   Paris   Capetown   Hong Kong   Montreal

Published in 2002 by
Prentice Hall
Pearson Education Asia Pte Ltd
23/25 First Lok Yang Road, Jurong
Singapore 629733

Pearson Education offices in Asia: *Bangkok, Beijing, Hong Kong,*
Jakarta, Kuala Lumpur, Manila, New Delhi, Seoul, Singapore, Taipei, Tokyo

Printed in Singapore

5 4 3 2 1
06 05 04 03 02

ISBN 0-13-008378-X

CONTENTS

TO ALL MY STUDENTS PAST, PRESENT AND FUTURE.
MAY LWIN

TO EVERYONE WHO MADE WORKING IN ADVERTISING SO EXCITING.
JIM AITCHISON

CLUE No.1: WHAT IS ISING?

WHAT IS ADVERTISING
AND HOW DO
COMPANIES USE IT?

Textbooks define advertising as part of the Promotional Mix, which consists of direct marketing, public relations, sales promotion and personal selling.

The Promotional Mix is one of the 4Ps in marketing, the others being Product, Pricing and Place.

Academics describe advertising as a key ingredient of promotional management using paid media space to convey a message, while clients and advertising agency practitioners view it simply as a means to communicate to consumers.

THE DIFFERENT
TYPES OF
ADVERTISING

STRATEGIC ADVERTISING builds brands. It does this by communicating brand values and product benefits. It is concerned with the long-term "positioning" of the brand, and building share of mind and share of market. It invites consumers to enjoy a relationship with the brand, and reassures existing users that the brand is still there for them.

TACTICAL ADVERTISING has a more urgent purpose. It is designed to bring the consumer into contact with the brand quickly. Generally tactical ads offer a short-term, special offer to spur the consumer into a same-day response.

RETAIL ADVERTISING by department stores, supermarkets and car dealers contains lots of special offers and stacks of merchandise. It is called "price-led" and the special offers are often referred to as "loss leaders": stock that the store is prepared to let go for little or no profit in order to attract the crowds. (Meanwhile the rest of its merchandise remains at normal prices.)

STRATEGIC ADVERTISING OVER 30 YEARS BY SINGAPORE AIRLINES HAS BUILT THE WORLD'S STRONGEST AIRLINE BRAND. BATEY ADS SINGAPORE

Most retailers follow convention; they believe the busier and messier their ads are, the more exciting they will look to consumers. However, other retailers believe their ads should be "strategic" as well and build a long-term personality for their business. Harrods and IKEA are two examples.

CORPORATE ADVERTISING is another form of strategic advertising, when a company runs a campaign to communicate its corporate values to the public. Corporate ads often talk about a company's heritage, a company's commitment to quality control, the launch of a company's new trademark or logo, or its concern for the environment. Sometimes corporate advertising has to correct public perceptions of the company; for example, oil companies might need to reassure the public about pollution control. Corporate advertising does not overtly "sell" — it is designed to win hearts and minds through gaining approval for the company's culture. It also works internally, influencing the morale of employees, as well as externally, on corporate customers.

BUSINESS TO BUSINESS ADVERTISING is when a company talks to other companies, usually in the pages of business magazines like *Forbes*, *The Economist* and *Fortune*. A new stock issue, new expansion plans, building corporate goodwill or the introduction of new corporate structures and services could all be reasons for business-to-business advertising.

PUBLIC SERVICE ADVERTISING (PSA) is on the increase. Governments and health authorities communicate messages about the link between cigarette smoking and cancer. Police departments warn motorists about drinking and driving. All kinds of institutions and charitable organisations crusade dozens of causes — refugees, the homeless, the handicapped, animal cruelty and violence against women and children.

Most advertising campaigns begin with strategic ads, supported later by tactical. Many brand-building experts believe that every ad is a strategic ad. As soon as the logo or trademark is included, the brand is "talking". Therefore, even a tactical ad or an ad in the Yellow Pages should have the tone and manner of the brand.

RETAIL ADVERTISING CAN
AS WELL AS SELL MERCHA
SINGAPORE'S TANGS USE (
TECHNIQUES AND HUMOU
CLUTTER AND WIN NEW C

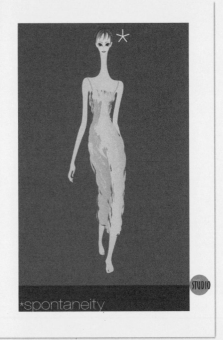

*spontaneity

STUDIO

The Tangs
Anniversary Sale
starts today

APPLICATION
FOR URGENT LEAVE

LD THE STORE'S IMAGE SE. CAMPAIGNS FOR TEMPORARY ILLUSTRATION CUT THROUGH THE OMERS. WORK SINGAPORE

Can't find your pet? Call SPCA's Lost & Found service at 287 5355. FRIENDS for LIFE

Can't find your pet? Call SPCA's Lost & Found service at 287 5355. FRIENDS for LIFE

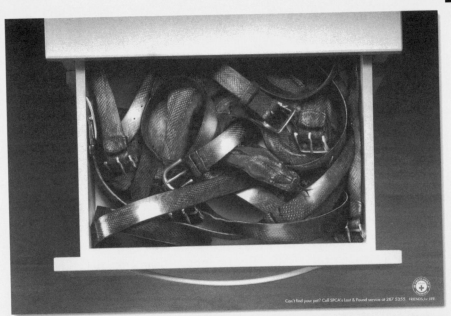

Can't find your pet? Call SPCA's Lost & Found service at 267 5355. FRIENDS for LIFE

THIS PUBLIC SERVICE CAMPAIGN WAS RUN BY THE SOCIETY FOR THE PREVENTION OF CRUELTY TO ANIMALS, PROMOTING ITS LOST & FOUND PET SERVICE.

LEO BURNETT SINGAPORE

WHAT ARE BRANDS?

Once, a brand simply meant a trademark, a legal name for a product. Many famous brands have existed for well over a century, like Lux, Gillette and Cadbury.

Some brands are companies like Cerebos, McDonald's, Mercedes-Benz, Nestlé, Nike, Shell, Singapore Airlines and Sony. And while some of these companies own many different brands, they always concentrate on one business. Coca-Cola the company always concentrates on beverages — Coke, Diet Coke, Sprite, Fanta, Schweppes, PowerAde, Hi-C, Minute Maid and Heaven & Earth.

Other companies like Procter & Gamble and Unilever own dozens of different brands that compete with each other in dozens of different categories — from household cleaners to hair shampoos, from detergents to foods. P&G owns around 70 international brands, makes 1,200 to 1,500 TV commercials a year to promote them, and spends US$4 billion running them. Unilever owns a staggering portfolio of brands which includes Lux soap to Lipton tea, while Colgate-Palmolive owns a lot more than Colgate toothpaste and Palmolive soap.

No matter who actually makes it, each brand stands for its own particular quality and consumers expect to experience that quality every time they purchase the brand.

But today, brands mean more than that. Brands have taken on personalities, just like the people who use them. Marketing experts will tell you that brands only exist in the minds of the consumers who use them. In fact, brands are not owned by the companies that manufacture them, but the consumers who buy them.

BRANDS: COMMUNITIES OF USERS

NEW YORK ADVERTISING AGENCY KIRSHENBAUM BOND describes a brand as a "Community of Users". When you buy a brand, you buy into a community of other users who share their love and trust of the brand with each other. Think about it. Mercedes-Benz is a different community from BMW, as Apple is from IBM. Nike is a community of athletes. Harley-Davidson is a blood brotherhood of users!

"BRANDS ARE THE BIGGEST THING IN THE WORLD"
STEVE HENRY

Steve Henry, founding partner of radical British agency Howell Henry Chaldecott Lury, tells us what brands mean: "What we are doing is building brands — and brands are arguably the biggest thing in the world, bigger than organised religion or politics as it is currently being played. Brands are what we identify with, so they are of massive importance in everybody's lives."

THE *COCA-COLA* MINISTRY OF ENJOYMENT CAMPAIGN REINFORCES THE BRAND'S LEADERSHIP BY USING LANGUAGE AND IMAGERY WITH WHICH THE TARGET AUDIENCE CAN RELATE. CREATED BY M&C SAATCHI SINGAPORE.

COCA-COLA IS A REGISTERED TRADE MARK OF THE COCA-COLA COMPANY.

16
WHAT DOES BRAND BUILDING MEAN?

Brands are the most important assets that companies have. Building the value of brands, and defending them against competitors, are what drive marketing.

In today's context, advertising doesn't "sell" products — it offers "brand relationships". It connects brands with new consumers or keeps brands connected to their existing consumers.

Here are some famous theories about the way that advertising helps build brands:

BOXES IN THE MIND In the 1950s at New York agency Ted Bates, Rosser Reeves formulated the theory that everyone has boxes in their minds for every product or service category, and each box can contain only two or three brand names. For example, if the toothpaste box were dominated by one name — Colgate — the consumer would most likely buy that brand. Advertising's job was to get the client's brand into as many mental boxes as possible. Reeves believed in "hard sell" ads that communicated a memorable Unique Selling Proposition for a product — something only that product could claim. A typical U.S.P. was *Cleans your breath while it cleans your teeth*, or *43 beans in every cup*. Reeves also believed in repeating the message as often as possible.

DISRUPTION is the revolutionary approach to marketing developed by Jean-Marie Dru of TBWA Worldwide. If companies don't create change, says Dru, change would create them. Dru argues that brands are in permanent transition and must be prepared to disrupt their own conventions to sustain themselves. Every advertising category has its conventions — toothpaste ads have shots of white teeth and beautiful faces, pizza ads have shots of gooey cheese, hair ads have shiny bouncy hair. Dru believes that brands must disrupt predictable normality and "reframe" themselves so they are seen in compelling new contexts. **THE UNTHOUGHT KNOWN** is the philosophy at work at London's Howell Henry Chaldecott Lury. The agency avoids playing to the rules of the market. It believes it should break rules and make the familiar unfamiliar. For example, it relaunched Britain's Automobile Association. The familiar roadside breakdown service was rebranded like the police, fire brigade and ambulance, and became *The Fourth Emergency Service.*

GOODBYE, U.S.P. HELLO, E.S.P.

Once, products did have genuine, tangible differences that were the central focus of advertising. Today, with products reaching higher standards of quality, differences are becoming fewer. Bartle Bogle Hegarty's John Hegarty says advertising now deals in perceived, intangible differences. "The U.S.P. has been replaced by the E.S.P., the Emotional Selling Proposition." Hegarty sees advertising as part of the manufacturing process. "We make ideas that make the difference between one brand and another. The emotional differences become the real differences."

Brands are made different emotionally through style, attitude, the way they are talked about, the way their commercials are shot, and the kind of music used. As Fallon Minneapolis art director Bob Barrie says, "What is the U.S.P. for Coke or Pepsi? Their advertising has become their U.S.P."

COMMERCIALS MUST REWARD VIEWERS

Professor John Philip Jones of Syracuse University, US, argues that effective campaigns offer rewards to viewers: "A thank you for spending thirty seconds in the company of the advertiser. This can take the form of emotional warmth, humour, entertainment, intrigue. There is no formula … but likeability is important."

They run and run and run and ru

SIMPLICITY MEANS COMMUNICATING ONE STRONG MESSAGE IN AN AD. TWO EXAMPLES OF BRAND-BUILDING POSTERS FROM DDB WORLDWIDE SINGAPORE: ONE ANNOUNCES THE ARRIVAL OF THE NEW VOLKSWAGEN BEETLE; THE OTHER COMMUNICATES VW RELIABILITY.

ADVERTISING: AN EXCHANGE OF ATTENTION FOR A REWARD

What works best — hard sell or soft sell? Andy Berlin, co-founder of legendary San Francisco agency Goodby, Berlin, Silverstein calls advertising a combination of entertainment and information transfer. "There's a machine that now puts PC technology and hard drives together with a zapper. You can now pause a 'live' television programme so that you can eat dinner, or make love, or go to the bathroom. You can fast forward thirty seconds and skip the commercial. Unless that commercial is so good that people want to watch it, it simply won't be watched. Advertising that is interesting and engaging and fun and valuable will always have a place."

HOW DO WE KNOW IF ADVERTISING WORKS?

Advertising is an essential part of mass media. We know that without it, mass media like television and radio, and perhaps our entire society, would be very different. Yet most of the time, advertisers don't really know how and if their advertising works.

In practical terms, the most important way to find out if advertising really works is to know what its objective is — and then "measure" the result after it has run. For example, the objective can be to tell the public about a new product, or to remind existing consumers about a price cut. Based on this objective, the advertiser can theoretically measure how effective a particular campaign is over a given time period. An increase in sales after the campaign has run is one way of measuring the advertising. Another is to "track" the awareness level of the brand among consumers by using research before and after the ads run.

In reality however, measuring advertising effectiveness is a complex task. This is because the effects of advertising may go beyond the simple task and result; sometimes, the effects will not be felt during the time period measured. Also, while this method allows the advertiser to measure the success of a campaign, it can only be used AFTER the campaign has been run. With so much ad expenditure on the line, advertisers want to ensure that the advertising is going to work BEFORE they spend millions of dollars on the campaign. This requires a variety of ad research techniques at different stages of the creative development. Depending on the importance of an ad campaign, and the investment involved in production and media, the advertising ideas and concepts can be tested for their effectiveness and impact on the target audience.

For example, nationwide ad campaigns for multinational accounts such as Pepsi and Burger King in the United States need to undergo extensive ad testing before they are produced while a simple one-page magazine ad in a local school magazine would hardly require an ad test. In undertaking ad research, the account planning or client service department will normally work with independent research firms, such as AC Nielsen and Frank Small and Associates. The research methods range from initial target market profiling, consumer research, to concept testing, pre- and posttesting, through to tracking studies.

HOW ADVERTISING
IS TESTED

Let's look at the major advertising test techniques that are used today to appraise the effectiveness and likely performance of a potential ad campaign.

For example, prior to the launch, the creative concept and the advertisements can be **pretested** at various stages of completion. Once the campaign has been launched, it can be **posttested** and tracked to yield consumer response data. Information gained from these tests can be used to aid advertisers' decision-making in areas such as advertising strategy, advertising budget directions and even media decisions.

PRETESTING

CONCEPT TESTING. This is carried out when the ad campaign is still under development. Colours, packaging, typeface, copy and design — literally every aspect of the advertisement can come under scrutiny at this stage. Evaluations are typically carried out in focus groups consisting of eight to ten people in a controlled setting. Participants are usually selected based on the demographics of the target audience for the ad. While this method leads to immediate observable results, it fails in the provision of statistical data and may produce biased results, as an actual home viewing environment with its inherent distractions cannot be ideally recreated.

INSIDE A FOCUS GROUP

Many advertisers insist that ideas be shown to panels of eight or ten consumers to find out whether the ideas will work in the marketplace. Usually these focus groups assemble in the early evening. They are shown rough print ads, drawn TV "storyboards" like big comic strips, and sometimes even mock videos called "animatics" where the drawn pictures are cut to music to make them more realistic. The advertiser and agency executives watch through a one-way window as a researcher leads the discussion.

Opinions about concept testing are sharply divided. Professor John Philip Jones never recommends using focus groups to predict campaign effectiveness. Australia's most respected social researcher Hugh Mackay condemns statistical analyses of audience reactions to television based on such tiny numbers of unscientifically selected people. "Advertisers are using pre-testing as a substitute for their own judgement," he argues.

Steve Henry uses research because "if we're going to go somewhere that nobody's been before, I want to know that the consumers are going to go there with me. But research, the way it's used currently in the industry, doesn't work. You have to have very sensitive research. It isn't about eight people saying I like this because it fits into my view of what's acceptable in the marketplace. You have to find the work that people are talking about when they leave the room. You have to find the piece of work that they're talking about most."

COMMERCIAL TESTING. This test requires a full mock-up of the final ad, which could consist of rendered artwork, or even the live-action staging of the TV commercial itself. Tests may be carried out both in a laboratory setting or on air. On-air testing would involve the placement of ads, both finished and those nearing completion, in actual TV programmes from selected test markets. The aim of this test is to find out whether the advertiser's intended message is getting across and whether the ad has elicited negative, unexpected reactions from its viewers. This test is cost effective as ads can be tested before they are completed. However, on-air tests cannot account for biases generated by the environment in which the ad is run and the user's level of product involvement.

POSTTESTING

INQUIRY TESTS. The effectiveness of an advertising campaign can be measured by the numbers of inquiries the advertiser receives. These inquiries could be the number of phone calls generated, or the number of reader cards or coupons returned. The numbers from the test can be used to track the effectiveness of the campaign over a period of time, even to test specific elements within the ad, and the effectiveness of the media in which it is run. In general, this test can answer questions on the campaign's cost effectiveness.

RECALL TESTS work on a basic premise that the higher the recall rate, the more memorable and thus more effective an ad is. Such tests seek to assess the performance and effectiveness of ads using both short-term and longer-term recall assessment.

RECOGNITION TESTS are essentially the same as recall tests, and examine the impressions that specific parts of an ad (such as design or copy) leave on consumers.

TEST MARKETING AND TRACKING STUDIES involve long-term testing of an ad campaign in markets that are demographically similar to the target market. This testing method allows the advantages of a controlled setting and the realism of an actual viewing environment. Test marketing studies the effects of an ad campaign on the consumer from the television set to the supermarket checkout counter. It can not only measure the results of the ad's performance, but also the long-term effects, such as the changes in consumer attitude, awareness, recall and interest towards the advertised product. The negative aspects of this method are the high cost of data collection, and the immense amount of time required.

DOES ADVERTISING LIE?

"THE VAST MAJORITY OF ADVERTISERS AND AGENCIES CONSIDER TRUTHFUL ADVERTISING TO BE IN THEIR OWN BEST INTEREST. IT IS A MATTER OF COMMON SENSE. UNTRUTHFUL ADVERTISING IS A FALSE PROMISE FOR A PRODUCT OR SERVICE. THEN WHAT YOU'VE GOT IS A DISSATISFIED CUSTOMER. NO BUSINESS CAN SURVIVE BY ACCUMULATING UNHAPPY CUSTOMERS."
LEONARD S. MATTHEWS, FORMER PRESIDENT OF THE AMERICAN ASSOCIATION OF ADVERTISING AGENCIES (4AS)

Advertising agency personnel need to know what is being done to keep advertising trustworthy. Many advertisers have policy standards to spell out the kind of advertising they want and will approve. Whole industries such as pharmaceuticals have advertising codes covering their fields.

Every country usually has a code of advertising standards which is endorsed and self-regulated by the advertising association. For example, Malaysia has a Malaysian Code of Advertising Practice that is overseen by ASAM (Advertising Standards Authority of Malaysia). Such associations usually comprise representatives from the agencies, media and advertisers. In the US, it is now a routine practice for advertising to be submitted to the agency lawyer and the client's legal department to evaluate the accuracy of the copy claims. However, this has not been as rigorously practised in the Asia-Pacific region. Ads regularly make it to print or television before anyone points out a problem.

So how can you learn about these codes and laws and help to ensure the ethical standards of your agency's ads? You can get hold of your country's codes for general guidance, and get specific help from the agency/client's legal counsel. You can also get some assistance from the publishers and broadcasters concerned. In many countries, the TV and radio stations must give their clearance based on their own set of codes before a commercial can run. Usually, the storyboard and copy need to be submitted long before production begins.

Despite the many ethical issues behind advertising, it is heartening to know that there are regulatory bodies constantly addressing this issue. Signs of their actions include the word "Advertisement" atop an advertorial that looks like a page of news, or the Surgeon General's warning on cigarette packets. More cases are also being heard in the courts to protect consumer interests. Such cases are bad public relations for the companies involved and force the mass media to safeguard against deceitful advertisements or those that overpromise. In the US, ads that use elderly, handicapped and minorities as spokespersons to make unbelievable claims have been toned down. However, in Asia, stereotypical, well-to-do heterosexual white Caucasian males or females are still being used in ads in the hope that their race will lift the product's "image".

Ultimately, it is up to the advertising agency, the advertisers and the consumer to question the validity of advertisements, and to question whether advertising is a good reflection of their company, or whether it creates the wrong societal values and beliefs. These are not simple issues and do not solicit right or wrong answers. One needs to be constantly aware of the complexities and sensitivities involved in the advertising messages. When in doubt about the ethical correctness of an ad message, always put yourself in the role of the consumer by asking questions such as, "Would I want my children or my mother to be persuaded by such a message?" and "Would this message mislead the average consumer in my community?"

ETHICAL CONCERNS IN ADVERTISING: THE DEBATE

WHAT THE CRITICS SAY: Many ethical concerns have been raised about advertising. In general, these issues deal with whether advertisers deceptively embellish or "puff" their commercials. Critics of such persuasive advertising advocate a more informational, fact-based form of advertising like those in newspaper classifieds, free of superfluous imagery that may mislead the consumer into buying things they do not need. They also point out that use of subliminal advertisements, or those occurring below a person's conscious threshold are akin to brainwashing. Many critics believe that advertising moulds people, and since advertisers have no moral obligations to society, wrong values may be passed on to viewers. Indeed, many studies show that consumers have given advertising the lowest rating among all businesses in terms of ethical standards. In particular, the young, elderly and "market illiterate" are the most affected audiences. Young children are affected because they do not yet know how to interpret what they see in advertising. (Recent claims that violent images in the mass media have led to more violent real-life incidents illustrate this point.) The elderly are also vulnerable because they receive most of their information from television and have few opportunities to substantiate advertisers' claims. And the "market illiterate" are people such as those with little education, who may not understand consumerism and how it works.

WHAT ADVERTISERS SAY: Advertisers claim a right to free speech. They say that advertising gives information to consumers, which in turn allows them a greater range in choice of products. They argue that consumers are not mindless beings, and are free to spend their money democratically in spite of advertising. It has also been argued that people know that advertisements are full of puffery and will not unduly take notice of any implausible claims. Advertisers claim that advertising merely reflects rather than moulds society. Advertising agencies claim that viewers want commercials to be entertaining as well, which makes all that excess visual imagery necessary. They also advocate that advertising need not abide by the standards of journalism such as having objectivity in writing. They argue that there can be no objectivity since the agency is selling a product for its client. Then there is the utilitarian argument that advertising helps to spur a capitalist society since advertising will benefit more people than it will harm.

There are many intricacies behind advertising. It is not simply the advertising agency that will be blamed for misleading claims, but the advertiser and the mass media as well. There are political and monetary issues behind these relationships that bring ethical boundaries into question. For example, can an agency reject the requests of a client for an unnecessarily violent commercial when there is money involved? Another ethical issue is the recently increased usage of advertorials and infomercials that look like genuine news. These are newspaper articles and television programmes where the distinction between paid advertising and "news" or "programme material" is blurred. For example, a company producing tea may have sponsored an article on tea and its benefits. Or, ads for recommended treatments and products for acne "just happen" to follow articles describing the condition.

Another issue is whether the media has a right to adjust its editorial content to suit the needs of its advertisers. What if a fashion magazine claims that the next fashion revolution will be floral prints, when the truth is that it is receiving a big advertising budget from a designer who has decided to adopt floral prints? What happens in these situations is that any opposing views may be suppressed in order for the publisher to appease the advertisers.

At the end of the day, it is plain common sense that if you lie to consumers, they will never buy your product again.

WHO DOES THE BEST ADVERTISING IN THE WORLD?

You don't have to work in New York or London to produce great advertising. Asian countries, along with Australia and New Zealand, have contributed some of the world's most famous campaigns. Outstanding work also comes from agencies in Brazil, Spain, Scandinavia and South Africa.

THE 3 GREAT ADVERTISING LEGENDS

BILL BERNBACH. Every budding young copywriter and art director should study the classic Bernbach campaigns. People in advertising still quote Bernbach as though he is alive and working down the corridor. In fact, many of his beliefs have become "creative law". Bill Bernbach revolutionised advertising in the 1960s. He made it wittier, more intelligent and occasionally very irreverent. Doyle Dane Bernbach New York produced the world's most imitated campaigns — Volkswagen and Avis. His idea for Avis, *We try harder*, provided a competitive edge for a company that was only second biggest. Bernbach's legendary art director Helmut Krone invented the famous DDB layout. Another DDB art director Roy Grace put a gorilla in a cage with a suitcase to prove how strong it was, used a funeral procession to advertise the economy of Volkswagen, and went on to create 25 of America's 100 all-time best commercials.

DAVID OGILVY was the founder of Ogilvy & Mather. Ogilvy based a lot of his agency philosophy on research. His most famous ads were for Rolls Royce — where the headline claimed the loudest noise in a Rolls was the clock on the dashboard — and the Hathaway Shirt campaign where the model wore an eye patch. Ogilvy was a Scotsman who entered advertising quite late in life. His passion for the business led him to develop very precise and hotly debated rules for effective creativity. Two of his most controversial edicts were that nobody buys from a comedian, and that white type reversed out of black is hard to read and therefore should never be used. However, few would argue with his principle that "the consumer isn't a moron, she's your wife". His books about advertising have been bestsellers for decades.

LEO BURNETT was not a New York man. He founded his agency in Chicago. One of his agency icons was an apple — when people told him he was crazy to open an agency and that he'd end up selling apples for a living, he replied that he would give them away first and put a bowl full of apples on the reception desk. His agency emblem — a hand reaching for the stars — invoked everyone to reach for the heights; that way, they wouldn't come up with a handful of mud. His most famous principle was "The Big Idea"; every campaign had to contain an enduring idea that would last for years and separate it from everything else. Sometimes "The Big Idea" would be a lovable, homespun character that led the campaign — Snap, Crackle and Pop, Tony the Tiger, Morris the Cat, the Jolly Green Giant. Other times it would be a branding idea like *Marlboro Country* and the cowboy, or *Fly the friendly skies* for United Airlines. Burnett's work always tapped into universal human values.

IS PUBLIC RELATIONS PART OF ADVERTISING?

Public relations is often confused with advertising. This is not surprising since they both communicate information to the public.

But public relations is different from advertising in two ways: it does not "buy" space in the media, nor does it "sell" something overtly.

Firstly, public relations takes place in a space that is uncontrolled and "free". Compare the placing of a paid advertisement for milk with a news report about spoilt milk. The ad is something within the authority of the company, but the news report is something that the company cannot predict.

Secondly, while advertising is meant to sell a product, public relations is primarily meant to explain a company's policies. Good PR can tide a company through retrenchment of staff, for example. Public relations can be used to determine the effects of a particular policy, and do damage control if it is not received well. ExxonMobil started a PR blitz to show how it had actually helped the local communities in Indonesia when news reports accused it of hiring the militia to protect its interests there.

The lines between advertising and public relations are sometimes blurred. Shell, for example, often takes out ads selling its environmentally friendly oil refining operations. However, most publicity is derived from news reports, which are seen as providing authoritative facts that the public can trust.

Can public relations be used to deceive the public into believing that a lousy product is good? No. Because PR depends so heavily on the goodwill of the news media, there are certain tasks that need to be undertaken in order to reach out to the press.

Let's look at some major functions of a publicist.

A publicist must be able to make your client's company newsworthy.

As a start, you need to develop a good working relationship with the editorial community. This rapport is needed to convince them that the company is able to provide what they want: information that the public will find informative and useful. One way is to position your client's staff as experts in their field. If your client is in the monetary business, for example, you can get analysts in the company to appear on news interviews involving market analysis.

You can also call for press conferences for the launch of a new product. In fact, any special event such as seminars and conferences can be newsworthy if the groundwork has been laid. Such preparation would include the actual planning and execution of the event, the preparation of media information such as press tips, and the setting up of appropriate press briefings. You can even submit news articles on the history and significance of the event to the press. The more "ink" you get for your client, the more successful you have been as a publicist.

A publicist needs to do research on a company's current standing among the public. This includes post-event research and analysis. Ratings may tell you how much reach you have attained, but whether people have interpreted your message as you intended it to be is another matter entirely. This is a public relations problem, and quite obviously good public relations is the solution.

Good publicists need a lot of imagination. Singapore's MDK generated worldwide publicity for Singapore Airlines when they arranged for London's famous Madame Tussaud's to display the figure of the Singapore Girl. In another classic PR exercise they announced on 31 March 1996 that a long-lost manuscript by the great British author Somerset W. Maugham had been found at Raffles Hotel. The news broke in the global media on the morning of 1 April — when everyone realised it was an April Fools' Day joke, much to the media's amusement.

A lone figure, stooped beneath a heavy burden, climbs through snow-covered peaks. Going in closer, we see it is an old man. Carefully he places a brick on a solitary tower he has constructed.

VO *What if the Great Wall of China had been left to just one person?*

The Mongol hordes are drawn up to attack. A canon ball rolls towards them and comes to rest harmlessly at a horse's feet.

VO *What if gunpowder had been kept a secret?*

A lone man is performing a Chinese lion dance. The empty lion wriggles like a giant worm in the heart of the deserted square.

VO *What if people were left to celebrate alone?*

A lone girl is playing table tennis by herself in an empty stadium.

VO *What if ping had no pong?*

A lone dragon boat racer sets down his oars so he can leap up and pound on the drum.

VO *What if people had to face every challenge on their own?*

The dragon boat is going round in circles on a vast lake.

VO *Only by helping each other can we be 1.2 billion times stronger. That's the power of the Internet. Netease. Power to the people.*

END WITH NETEASE LOGO AND LINE: *Power to the people.*

AN EMOTIONALLY POWERFUL BRAND-BUILDING CAMPAIGN FOR CHINESE INTERNET PORTAL, NETEASE, CREATED BY SAATCHI & SAATCHI BEIJING.

要是节日只有一人庆祝？

任何庆祝，只有更多人参与，才能拥有更多的欢乐。网络时代每个人的欢乐都能变成大家的欢乐，因为互联网把所有人联在一起。当所有有人同参与、共分享时，12亿人的力量谁可估量？网易致力于推动中国互联网发展。率先开发出全中文搜索引擎，免费电子邮件系统，网上虚拟社区等先进技术，建造中国

网易新一代搜索引擎——网聚资讯的动力
这日网易推出新一代搜索引擎，在国内第一采用并开放式目录管理方式，期望各界专业人士参与目录编辑，确保按全搜索，详情登陆网易查询。

互联网的平台，然而都没有超百万的共同参与，我们又如何创造出网页面浏览量2,400万登记用户590万，聊天室34,000人，网时共用的人业绩？感谢大家的参与。期待更多人参与进来，与我们一起共建中国互联网的美好未来。 **网聚人的力量**

網易 **NETEASE**
www·163·com

· 本记录载止于2000年6月30日

要是面对挑战 都是孤军奋战？

任何挑战，唯有更多同伴支持，才能临危不惧，赢得胜利。网络时代你地不会再孤军奋战，因为互联网所有人联在一起。当所有人同参与、共分享，12亿人的力量谁可估量？网易致力于推动中国互联网发展。率先开发出全中文搜索引擎，免费电子邮件系统，网上虚拟社区等先进技术，建造中国

网易奥运站点(http://anyun.163.com)火速开通
网易最新最真正互动，人人参与的奥运站点。
与全国有线电视联播网携手热烈，同步互动。
看参与，才够high！详情登录网易直播。

互联网的平台，然而都没有超百万的共同参与，我们又如何创造出网页面浏览量2,400万登记用户590万，聊天室34,000人，网时共用的人业绩？感谢大家的参与。期待更多人参与进来，与我们一起共建中国互联网的美好未来。 **网聚人的力量**

網易 **NETEASE**
www·163·com

· 本记录载止于2000年6月30日

WHERE C

CLUE No. 2:
N YOU FIT
INTO ADVERTISING?

If you like a quiet life with a nine-to-five job, don't go into advertising! Advertising is a high-pressure profession. It can be exciting, challenging and enormously inspiring. It can also be exhausting and depressing. In fact, multiple deadlines, day after day, cause some people to burn out early. It doesn't help when advertising people are called "hucksters", or are accused of manipulating minds. That's why it makes sense to learn as much as possible about advertising and the careers available before making a commitment.

If you *do* want a career in advertising, it is a good idea to start by evaluating your strengths and weaknesses. In advertising agencies, there's room for different types of individuals — in client management, creative, media analysis and buying, and in research. Many are rewarded and happy to be doing what they enjoy.

Large agencies are likely to be more structured, with several levels of account management and various department managers and specialists. In the small agencies, staff often wear different hats — servicing the clients, creating the idea *and* buying the media. So the content of the job differs by agency size. Many advertising people think it is best to begin in a small agency so you can experience and understand all the different disciplines quickly.

HOW DO
ADVERTISING AGENCIES
WORK?

The first advertising agents were sales agents, selling media space to advertisers. As part of the sale, they would come up with ideas for the advertiser as well.

Over the years, agencies became more sophisticated, offering specialised communications services to marketing firms in executing a marketing plan. Today's ad agencies are very much partners in the client's marketing functions, involved in areas beyond just advertising. Product development and consumer research are often agency responsibilities.

HOW DO AGENCIES EARN THEIR INCOME?

Media owners traditionally paid advertising agencies a 15% commission for any time or space purchased on behalf of their clients. The plus point of this fixed remuneration system was that agencies had to fight on quality since they could not compete on price. The commission system has, however, been a subject of much debate. For example, since the agency only received payment from commissionable media, it may not actively push for other communication channels, such as direct mail, even though it might have been a more efficient option. Also, under this system the advertiser was seldom appraised of the precise use of his advertising dollars.

To solve this problem, the commission system has often been modified to encompass a fixed-fee system and cost-plus agreements. In a fee-commission system, the agency may reduce the amount of commission it receives and substitute the remainder with an agreed upon payment by the advertiser for predetermined services. This agreement may be based on the cost-plus system where the agency is paid for work done plus an agreed upon profit margin. This also allows for extremely explicit and transparent tracking of the advertiser's dollars.

Advertisers are now clamouring for agencies' fees to be tied to the success (or failure) of the campaign it puts out, thereby increasing their accountability. The latest trend is a move towards an incentive-based system. Under this system, agencies may be paid based on their success on achieving certain goals, such as increased sales. In reality, many advertisers typically work out a payment system that combines the commission, fixed-fee and incentive-based systems. Agencies need to make a profit like any other businesses, and proper compensation for their efforts will no doubt return a corresponding amount of effort.

MEDIA BUYING SERVICES

Of late, there has been a rise in independent companies that specialise in media buying. Some even assist in the planning of media strategy. Because these firms buy such large amounts of time and space, they receive large discounts and can save smaller agencies and clients money on media purchases.

NO CONTRACTS, PLEASE — IT'S ONLY ADVERTISING!

Even though clients will spend millions of dollars with an advertising agency, their contract is very often simply in the form of a letter. Called a "Letter of Appointment", it confirms the agency's appointment and the fact that bills will be settled within 30 days for media and 45 days for production. In most cases, notice of termination can be as short as 30 days, after which the client is free to take all the work produced by that agency to a new agency.

WHAT ARE THE
DIFFERENT TYPES OF
AGENCIES?

Global advertisers generally use big multinational agencies with global networks of offices. Local agencies usually service local clients. As a general rule, most advertisers like to dance with agencies that have the same size feet.

Around the world there are two types of agencies: the full-service agencies and the specialist agencies. **Full service agencies** offer an entire range of services, starting with advertising strategy formulation, creating the full-fledged advertising and promotions campaign, producing it and working out the media plan. This group includes multinational agencies like BBDO, Ogilvy & Mather and McCann-Erickson, as well as the bigger local agencies like Britain's Mother and St. Luke's, Australia's Brown Melhuish Fishlock, Singapore's Crush, Ace:Daytons and 10AM Communications, and Taiwan's Ideology.

On the other hand, **specialist agencies** are mainly local. Of late, some have become fashionably known as the "boutique" agencies and tend to concentrate on small creative jobs.

There are various rates of success in terms of consistent growth, profitability and client retention. Mostly though, today's successful agencies need high standards of creativity and a good deal of marketing sophistication.

WHY IS AMERICAN ADVERTISING CALLED "MADISON AVENUE" WHEN ALL THE AGENCIES ARE SOMEWHERE ELSE?

WHERE IT ALL BEGAN... PARK ROW, NEW YORK, SEEN HERE IN 1895.

(REPRODUCED FROM THE BYRON COLLECTION, BY KIND PERMISSION OF THE MUSEUM OF THE CITY OF NEW YORK.)

In 1897, a little New York street called Park Row was the headquarters of the advertising business. At 38 Park Row, George Batten crammed his agency into a 12-foot by 14-foot office. He ran an ad that said: I WANT MORE BUSINESS. Meanwhile at 39–41 Park Row, naval veteran James W. Thompson was getting plenty of it. Within a few short years his agency would be America's biggest.

In 1902, former department store advertising manager Alfred W. Erickson opened an agency that later became McCann-Erickson. In 1928, the George Batten Company merged with Barton, Durstine & Osborn and became BBDO. A year later, two Batten executives, William Benton and Chester Bowles, left to start their own agency – Benton & Bowles – which is now part of

D'Arcy. Another Batten executive, Ted Bates, opened his agency a few years later.

Madison Avenue had been a street of trolley tracks, brownstone houses and block after block of department stores called Ladies' Mile. In 1917, J. Walter Thompson moved to 244 Madison Avenue and the rest is history. (Not only did JWT relocate; romance was in the air. A JWT Cincinnati copywriter Helen Lansdowne came to town, married her boss Stanley Resor, and together they led the agency for the next 50 years!)

Madison Avenue boomed. BBDO was there, so was McCann-Erickson. Even the legendary Doyle Dane Bernbach opened at 350 Madison Avenue — in the attic, the so-called penthouse floor. (The elevators stopped one floor below!)

Yet, despite all the hype, more agencies were on Fifth Avenue than Madison. Perhaps because Fifth Avenue already had an image of upscale retail stores, Madison became the street of fast-talking "hucksters" and the home of the three-martini lunch.

By 1996, over 35,000 agency employees earned US$2,514,942,668 on New York's "Madison Avenue".

NOT A MAC IN SIGHT! THE ART DEPART-MENT OF McCALL'S MAGAZINE, 1912.

(REPRODUCED FROM THE BYRON COLLECTION, BY KIND PERMISSION OF THE MUSEUM OF THE CITY OF NEW YORK.)

GETTING STARTED IN ADVERTISING

Three major departments are involved in taking an advertisement from concept to reality. The account service people are those who liaise directly with the company putting out the advertising campaign; the creative department is where the ad actually takes shape; and the media department which decides where the ads will run and books them with the media. Larger agencies also have a planning department in charge of research and developing the strategic direction of accounts.

THE ACCOUNT
SERVICE DEPARTMENT

Known also as account management, this is the department that handles accounts, takes the role of marketing for the agency and oversees the client's business. Account service people are also known as "suits", named after their relatively formal attire, or "contact persons", and represent the front line that services the agency's clients. Most account service departments consist of driven, business-oriented staff whose functions are to service the client efficiently, to retain (and increase) the account's business and to see that the agency makes money. The account management department contacts the client almost daily and is responsible for a number of tasks, including formal presentations and obtaining approval for agency's output.

Within the agency, the client services department is seen as the client's representative. The account service personnel communicate the advertising strategy and the directions from the client to all departments within the agency. They are responsible for initiating assignments within the agency, providing deadlines, outlining budgets and ensuring that work is consistent with strategy before the advertising campaign is presented to the client. The client service people tend to interact with all departments within the agency, including creative, media, production, and finance. Their job is to focus the agency's effort to enable the agency's departments to perform at their optimum.

ACCOUNT SERVICE CAREER LADDER

CLIENT SERVICE HEAD
ACCOUNT DIRECTOR (A/D)
ACCOUNT MANAGER (A/M)
ACCOUNT SUPERVISOR (A/S)
ACCOUNT EXECUTIVE (A/E)
JUNIOR ACCOUNT EXECUTIVE (A/E)

When an advertiser deals with an agency, he prefers to talk to one person or an agency team. However, agencies find it a business necessity for account service staff to work on more than one account.

The entry position in most agencies is a junior or trainee account executive or A/E. The A/E's responsibility is to be the client's representative within the agency and vice versa. An A/E is the go-between for day-to-day contact between the two parties. The client looks upon the account representative as the person who should interpret his ideas and desires to the agency. The agency expects the account representatives not only to keep it informed of the client's wishes, but also to protect it by issuing written reports after every meeting. These call reports record every important client-agency meeting and the client's approval of each step in the relationship. Items to be submitted for approval include schedules, copy, layout, artwork and proofs. The agency and client must work as a team to enable the client's products to be promoted successfully. It is crucial that the account management maintains a good relationship with the client. In fact, survey research has indicated that agency-client longevity is more dependent on strong personal relationships than any other factors.

The account executive should be dynamic, adaptable and have loads of initiative. He or she should be able to deliver fresh and creative perspectives about the product in relation to the marketplace. Good account executives are much, much more than "bag carriers". They orchestrate the agency as a team and add significant value and marketing insight to the problem at hand while continually working towards a long-term vision.

The job of an A/E is particularly suitable for those with strong writing, presentation and conversational skills. He or she should also have a firm grasp of marketing and all aspects of advertising, and be in touch with market and consumer trends. Although paper qualifications are not mandatory, many of today's account executives in multinational agencies often hold marketing or other business diplomas or degrees. Effective A/Es are quickly promoted to supervisory level as A/Ss and A/Ms. At these levels, the account service personnel are involved not just in the day-to-day servicing of accounts, but in agency presentations, writing strategies and research. Account managers report to the account director or in small agencies, directly to the client service head. The account directors usually oversee a portfolio of major and smaller accounts. They are very experienced and are instrumental in formulating strategy, as well as ensuring the profitability of their accounts. Above the account director is the group account director and often the client service head, reporting directly to the agency managing director. They are usually in charge of a large group of accounts, running their group or department while handling agency management issues. Unless there is a new business department in an agency, these director-level personnel often spearhead the agency's new business presentations or "pitches". In most multinational agencies, they also co-ordinate account activities at regional or even international level.

The good news is that *both* young men and women can choose an account service career. In fact, many more women than men work in account service and often reach the top jobs — some have become managing directors of their agencies.

WHAT IS A "CALL REPORT"?

The account representative is charged with the job of getting the client's approval on the creative work and media schedules. The decisions made at meetings are recorded in a call report that is intended for the agency's permanent records. The report also records the deadlines agreed by the client and the agency. When the creative department proceeds with work on a particular brief, the account representative must get the client's approval for each piece of copy and every visual, layout and finished piece of artwork. It is the account representative's job to ensure everything reaches the client by the promised deadline and at the agreed cost. A call report dictated by the agency account representative should immediately follow every discussion with the client. A copy of this report is mailed to the client and another given to the agency executive in charge of production. If the client feels that the account representative has misinterpreted his instructions, he will contact the account service department and make corrections. This call report system prevents mistakes and misunderstandings. This policy is strictly adhered to by ad agencies, even when the client occupies space in the same building.

WHAT IS "PLANNING"?

Account planning is a process of discovery that lets the agency understand more about the brand and more about the consumer's relationship with the brand. The purpose of planning is to find new ways to fit the consumer and the brand together. Planning is like detective work, picking up clues from the market and applying them to solve strategic problems. Planners work independently, and bring back their understanding of the marketplace to the client and the agency. The planners can then help work out the marketing and advertising strategies and co-ordinate the use of research.

Because account service staff are so busy servicing clients, they usually don't have hours to spend on such analytical work. Planners also work closely with creative staff, helping to shape their ideas so the advertising precisely answers market needs. Many famous award-winning campaigns have been the result of planning.

Stanley Pollitt first pioneered planning in the mid-1960s at London agency Pritchard Wood Partners. When he opened Boase Massimi Pollitt (BMP) in 1968, planning became the cornerstone of the agency. BMP has trained a generation of planners and the methodology has spread to many other agencies. Unfortunately, not all planners practise account planning the way it was intended; and as a result the discipline has many critics.

THE CREATIVE DEPARTMENT

This is the factory that makes the agency's "product" — ideas that it sells to clients, newspaper and magazine ads, TV and radio commercials, posters and brochures. Most creative departments are either deathly quiet (because everybody is out working on assignments, or staring at the walls waiting for inspiration) or completely chaotic, with people shouting and screaming at each other.

A COPYWRITER'S CAREER LADDER

EXECUTIVE CREATIVE DIRECTOR
CREATIVE DIRECTOR
HEAD OF COPY
CREATIVE GROUP HEAD
SENIOR COPYWRITER
COPYWRITER
JUNIOR COPYWRITER

The most important requirement is the ability to write — not to copy what others write, but to create original, fresh ideas. These days, copywriters often think up ideas without any words at all because many ads are visual not verbal. Copywriters are usually teamed with art directors. They solve problems together, sharing the job of coming up with pictures and headlines.

Once, copywriters were expected to dash off slick headlines and body copy for print ads, or the scripts and voice-over copy for TV. Today, advertising demands a more subtle use of words. Great advertising copywriters are "ideas" people who can solve communications problems; their ability with words is matched by their knowledge of how people will respond to different messages and stimuli. The best copywriters in advertising read lots of books, watch all kinds of movies, have wide musical tastes, and turn their minds into "attics", storing up all kinds of impressions and experiences from life.

When they first start work in an agency, young copywriters are usually given small print ads to do, maybe some simple radio or TV. No matter how unimportant the job may look — a mailbox leaflet, an ad in the phone book, a retail ad on radio — every job is a chance to shine. Many young writers practise the "50 Boxes" method of creating ideas: they force themselves to do 50 ideas for every assignment, knowing that eventually their imaginations will come up with better and better ideas. Long hours go with the job. But the best young writers earn quick recognition from their peers. Some can boast a string of awards and a substantial monthly salary while still in their 20s.

Creative directors or their deputies hire budding copywriters. They will be looking for people who can think up fresh ideas. Having a degree or diploma is not essential. Preference will always be given to natural born writers. There are no colleges for writers. Creativity can be harnessed, but not taught.

Candidates who can demonstrate an understanding of what advertising is all about, and how words can work with pictures, will always be given a chance.

Progress is based on talent and achievement, not seniority. Most copywriters learn their craft on the job, watching how senior writers and art directors go about doing things. Once a copywriter has built a "book" of good work and won some awards, he will have something to show other creative directors. **JUNIOR COPYWRITERS** generally become full-fledged copywriters within two years. (If they don't, then perhaps they should think of changing their job, or their career.)

COPYWRITERS AND SENIOR COPYWRITERS are assigned to a group of accounts. They "learn" each account — what the culture of the brand is, what ads have been done already, what kind of ideas are appropriate for the brand and what other brands in the same category are doing.

CREATIVE GROUP HEADS are in charge of the ideas produced by individual writer-art director teams. They act as filters so that weak ideas are arrested before clients see them. Group heads are responsible to creative directors.

HEAD OF COPY is a rare title these days. Originally, the head of copy supervised the work of copywriters, edited their copy and called for rewrites.

CREATIVE DIRECTORS are either "copy based" or "art based". The CD's responsibilities are to improve the agency's creative output, lead and inspire the creative teams, present concepts to clients and help persuade them to buy the ideas. Sadly, most CDs stop doing actual work; they have no time to create. Instead, they nurture others. Given their experience, they are frequently invited to judge award shows and often become spokesmen for their agencies and the industry.

In bigger agencies where three or four creative directors are needed, one will be the executive creative director.

Many copywriters, like David Ogilvy, open their own agencies. According to stories, even when Ogilvy & Mather had become a vast international agency, Ogilvy still referred to himself as a copywriter.

AN ART DIRECTOR'S CAREER LADDER

EXECUTIVE CREATIVE DIRECTOR
CREATIVE DIRECTOR
HEAD OF ART
CREATIVE GROUP HEAD
SENIOR ART DIRECTOR
ART DIRECTOR
JUNIOR ART DIRECTOR OR VISUALISER

Unlike copywriters who have to be able to write, art directors don't have to be able to draw. However, art directors do need formal art college training or a diploma in graphic arts. Young art directors will be expected to have practical typographic, layout and design skills.

Many young art directors start as visualisers, rendering layouts for senior art directors and producing mock-ups of ads on Apple Macs for clients to approve. Once they have proved they can come up with visual ideas and produce professional layouts, they will be matched with young copywriters as creative teams.

Young art directors are expected to be aware of the latest techniques and technology. They can study layout styles and typography in magazines like *Archive*, and cutting edge cinematographic and editing techniques on TV reels like *Shots* and *Campaign Screen*. (Some, however, become so obsessed with execution that they lose sight of conceptualising.) Like great young copywriters, great young art directors have minds like attics: they will soak up everything around them — new movies as well as classics, images from real life, even the way people walk and talk. Some will have a natural ability to write, too; art directors who can write their own headlines frequently become creative directors.

Successful young art directors can become senior art directors and later creative group heads. A head of art is frequently found in many agencies with a British structure; the head of art is always an accomplished, respected art director who upholds the agency's visual standards, and acts as a referee when matters of taste and judgement become issues. The head of art will usually nurture and supervise younger art directors.

Many creative directors are from an art background. Some, like Paul Arden of Saatchi & Saatchi London, eventually leave agency life and become film directors.

BE A SPONGE
The best advertising people, says Graham Fink, are engaged in a constant process of observing, storing and connecting. Fink made the transition from agency creative to film director, and was president of Britain's Design & Art Direction in 1996. He is an icon for young British creatives.

"Be a sponge — go and soak up as much information as you can. Read books, read magazines, go to the theatre, go to the cinema, go swimming, go walking, read a book about bringing up a dog, find out about glassblowing. The Internet is like the greatest encyclopaedia in the world. There are too many advertising people who just sit in an office and say we've got to do an ad. The worst thing they can do is look in the award books. All that stuff's been done."

Leo Burnett said: "Curiosity about life in all of its aspects, I think, is still the secret of great creative people."

CREATIVE TEAMS

Once agency copywriters worked in the copy department, and art directors worked in the art department. They rarely spoke to each other. Often the two departments were located on separate floors. Bill Bernbach pioneered the idea of writers and art directors working as a team in the same room. Paired like married couples, some teams stay together for years, moving from one agency to the next, even opening their own agency together.

Not everyone agrees that creative teams are a good idea.

Australian David Droga, the young executive creative director of Saatchi & Saatchi London, calls it a dangerous scenario. "Nothing can outdo a great team, but sometimes similar personalities clash, sometimes somebody won't want to voice an opinion because it might sound foolish. If you're stuck with the wrong partner, it can be an awkward situation, especially if the teaming has been thrust on you." Droga prefers different people working with each other, "so they experience new people, new things."

CAREERS IN CREATIVE CRAFTS

Not everyone in the creative department aspires to be a writer, art director or creative director.

ILLUSTRATORS. Visualisers who draw storyboard frames and illustrations for press ads often discover they have far greater potential as fulltime freelance illustrators. Specialised advertising illustrators with exceptional talent often earn much more than they might have done as art directors.

THE POWER OF A GREAT ILLUSTRATION: THIS IMAGE OF UNCLE SAM CALLING AMERICANS TO VOLUNTEER FOR MILITARY SERVICE WAS CREATED IN 1917 BY JAMES MONTGOMERY FLAGG. ONE HUNDRED YEARS LATER, IT CAN STILL RALLY THE AMERICAN PEOPLE.

TYPOGRAPHERS. Typography is a lost art. It has ceased to be a trade skill available only from a specialist supplier. But while everyone it seems can operate a Mac, some do it better than others. Young designers who are exceptionally gifted typographers will still find opportunities to exploit their talent in a big agency creative department with a heavy print output.

ART BUYERS have a rare skill. They can "see" the art director's vision for an ad, and help bring it to fruition by choosing the right illustrator or photographer. They are also responsible for negotiating the best possible rates and keeping the job within budget.

A **TRAFFIC MANAGER**, assisted by traffic clerks, has her finger on the pulse of the creative department. She will know the status of every job in the agency. When a job comes in to her domain, she will check that the deadlines are reasonable. If they aren't, she will negotiate for more time. But once she agrees to them, she will be responsible for meeting them. Her job qualifications include knowledge of all the various production processes, management skills and either a lot of patience or a formidable temper.

STUDIO MANAGERS supervise every aspect of the studio's output, ensuring that artwork is finished to the required standard on time for production. In the computer age, the studio manager's role is often merged with the print production manager's duties.

PRINT PRODUCTION MANAGERS supervise the production standards of all the agency's newspaper and magazine ads. They are also responsible for printing brochures, annual reports and posters — from calling for quotes, choosing printers, selecting paper stock and negotiating prices, to quality control of films, colour separations and printing.

A **BROADCAST PRODUCTION MANAGER** or **HEAD OF BROADCAST** leads the television and radio production department. Some very big agencies even have television commercial directors on staff. The entry-level job in broadcast is production assistant, rising to agency producer. The job entails gathering quotes from film companies and recording studios, casting the talent, being on location to assist with production, attending voice recording and editing sessions, and ensuring that the work does not go over budget and is delivered on time. Many experienced producers eventually leave to work in production houses where their knowledge of agency procedures gives them a great advantage.

IS THERE LIFE
AFTER ADVERTISING?

American novelist **F. Scott Fitzgerald** was a copywriter at Barron Collier, writing posterads for streetcars. For an Iowa steam laundry he came up with the slogan, *We'll keep you clean in Muscatine.* Poet **Ogden Nash** worked there, too.

Joseph Heller worked in the promotions department at Remington Rand before writing *Catch-22.*

Author **Salman Rushdie** was once a copywriter at Ogilvy & Mather, London. Reportedly he dashed off lines like, *A Mars a day helps you work, rest and play.*

Twice winner of the Booker Prize for Literature, **Peter Carey** was a top Australian copywriter and ran his own agency in Sydney, McSpedden Carey.

Star of TV's *The Munsters*, **Fred Gwynne**, was a copywriter at JWT New York. In the same agency, TV commercials director **George Roy Hill** went on to make *Butch Cassidy & The Sundance Kid* and *The Sting.*

THE MEDIA DEPARTMENT

Once, every agency had a department that planned where, when and how campaigns would run. The media department produced a schedule for the client's approval, negotiated rates with the media, and then executed the plan. This department has almost disappeared in many agencies because media functions are now in the hands of specialist media houses called media brokers.

For a media jobseeker, a marketing foundation would give you an edge. More importantly, statistical and numerical skills would definitely be an asset. Aspiring media personnel sometimes fear that the media department has become all numbers and no heart. With the introduction of computers, media people have become ever more dependent on number crunching to chart a campaign's path. However, the media department is an important creative facet in the campaign development trail, and the human element is as important as any scientific rationale in any media function.

THE MEDIA PLANNING PROCESS

Media planning involves the process of designing a scheduling plan that shows how advertising time and space will contribute to the achievement of marketing objectives.

MEDIA STRATEGY:
1. SELECTING TARGET AUDIENCE.
2. SPECIFYING MEDIA OBJECTIVES.
3. SELECTING MEDIA CATEGORIES.
4. BUYING MEDIA.

THE MEDIA PLANNING PROCESS

MARKETING STRATEGY

AD STRATEGY

AD OBJECTIVES | AD BUDGET | MESSAGE STRATEGY | MEDIA STRATEGY

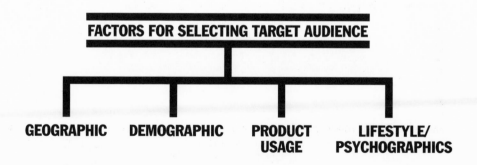

FACTORS FOR SELECTING TARGET AUDIENCE

GEOGRAPHIC | DEMOGRAPHIC | PRODUCT USAGE | LIFESTYLE/ PSYCHOGRAPHICS

GENERAL MEDIA INFORMATION

REACH — Percentage of target audience exposed to an ad at least once during a certain time frame (usually four weeks)

FREQUENCY — Average number of times an ad reaches the target audience in a four-week period

WEIGHT — Gross rating points, or GRPs, indicate the amount of gross weight that a particular ad schedule is capable of delivering.

GRPs = Reach(R) x Frequency(F)

DETERMINING GRPs
- GRPs are the sum of all vehicl ratings in a media schedule.
- Rating: proportion of the targe audience presumed to be exposed to a single occurrenc of an ad vehicle in which the brand is advertised.

CONTINUITY — How advertising is allocated during the course of an ad campaign

- Continuous schedule
- Pulsing
- Flighting

COST —

COST CONSIDERATIONS
Cost of reaching target audience of 1,000

COST CONSIDERATIONS
Cost-Per-Thousand (CPM)
Target Market (TM)

$$CPM = \frac{ad\ cost}{\#\ of\ contacts\cdot}$$

$$CPM-TM = \frac{ad\ cost}{\#\ of\ TM\ contacts}$$

*in thousands

FACTORS INFLUENCING REACH
- More people are reached when a schedule uses multiple media
- Number and diversity of media used

SAMPLE MAGAZINE EXPOSURES

TARGET AUDIENCE

Week	A	B	C	D	E	F	G	Total Exposures
1		x			x		x	3
2			x		x		x	3
3	x	x		x				3
4					x	x	x	3
Total Exposure	1	2	1	2	3	1	2	

THE CONCEPT OF ERPs
- How often the target audience has an opportunity to be exposed
- Effective Reach is based on the idea that an ad schedule is effective only if it reaches members of target audience

HOW MANY EXPOSURES?
- Three-Exposure Hypothesis: Minimum number of exposures needed for advertising to be effective is three
- Efficiency-Index Procedure: Media schedule that generates the most exposure value per GRP

THREE METHODS OF SCHEDULING

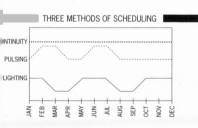

SHELF-SPACE MODEL OF ADVERTISING
- Consumers' first exposure to an ad is the most powerful
- Achieving a high level of weekly reach for a brand should be emphasized over acquiring heavy frequency
- Reach target audience continuously rather than sporadically

COST CONSIDERATIONS
- Measures cost efficiency, not effectiveness
- Vehicles within a particular medium are usually compared on the same basis but not across media

58

MEDIA CAREER LADDER

- MEDIA DIRECTOR
- MEDIA GROUP HEAD
- MEDIA PLANNER
- MEDIA BUYER
- MEDIA ASSISTANT

As the name suggests, people in the media department are in charge of anything that has to do with the media. Most people start off work in this department as a media assistant to the media buyer and planner — two of the most important roles in the media department. The job scope of these includes the collection of data regarding the demographics of the various media users and the buying of media space where the ad is to be run. These tasks are all interrelated, as is the media department's relation with the account service and creative departments.

The first thing the media department does upon receiving a request for a schedule is to decide where the ads should go and how the campaign should be run. This is the work of the media planner. An understanding of the client's business and the campaign objectives is very important. The target market and the type of product being sold have to be considered, as well as the time period for the campaign launch and its aggressiveness over this period; all have to be planned within budget considerations.

Once the planning has been done, the spotlight will turn on the media buyer. The buyer needs to have a good rapport with the media owners for several reasons. Media space, like shares, is a traded commodity with advertising spaces often available at discounted rates. As such, the price of media can fluctuate. The job of the media buyer is to be aware of these trends through a good working relationship with the media personnel. The buyer ultimately makes the purchase.

The media group head's position is where good planners and buyers will eventually end up. It is the group head's duty to collate the information his team has collected and call regular meetings so that the relevant people involved with the campaign will be kept updated. This way, the creative department will be able to work within practical boundaries and not come up with fantastic ads that cannot be executed, and the account service team can use the media department's data to argue the case for the creative team's efforts. The team effort will become more streamlined since the creative and account teams can defend their selected strategy and more importantly, state why it will work.

Experience is what counts in the media director's position. You can only expect to reach this post after arduously working in the trade for many years. It is the director's job to see that the numbers act as guidelines rather than rules to be followed to a T. The numbers may point one way, but the director's gut feeling, honed from years of experience, may reveal a different take on these same numbers. The director's role is to lead the department, interface with other senior management people, and be involved in business development.

A CRASH COURSE IN MEDIA:
THE PROS AND CONS

TELEVISION: Running ads through broadcast television can result in an impressive reach since television enjoys wide appeal. Furthermore, television is something that can be merchandised. This means that the "sell" can be done in ways other than by inserting an ad into a particular time slot. The aspect that gives broadcast television its greatest advantage is also its Achilles' heel. Having an extended reach means that it is virtually impossible to target a specific audience. The biggest void may be more upscale consumers who tend to watch less television. One solution to this is to advertise on cable TV. However, cable TV, in polar opposite to broadcast television, has a much smaller reach. Broadcast television does allow the advertiser to select the broadcast time slots, which can allow some limited viewer targeting.

RADIO: This is one medium that is excellent for targeting a fixed audience, which translates to increased frequency when the ad is run many times over

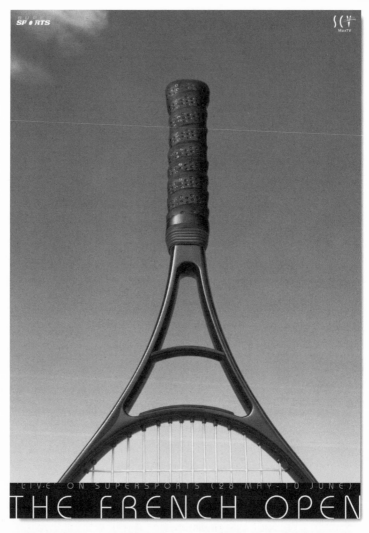

THE FRENCH OPEN

LIVE ON SUPERSPORTS (28 MAY-10 JUNE)

THE EIFFEL TOWER WAS CREATED OUT
FRENCH OPEN TELECAST ON SINGAPOR
REQUIRE A LOT OF MONEY, JUST A LOT

a space of time. Individual programmes have loyal listeners, which allows for a specific audience to be targeted. The programmes themselves can also be merchandised the same way as broadcast television. Radio is about the fastest way to communicate a message to an audience. The downside is that most people leave the radio on without actively listening to it, which has to be taken into account when planning effective communications to a wider audience.

MAGAZINES: Magazines allow the greatest amount of targeted advertising simply because there is such a wide range of periodicals covering all kinds of subject matter. The content of the magazine can help to intensify the product sell through advertorials, where an article in the magazine may directly or indirectly refer to the product that is to be advertised. Magazines also have an extended life because they are often passed on to many other readers — and this means multiple readings of the same advertisement. Magazine advertisements can be more detailed since readers have time to mull over them. Magazines also offer the best reproduction of pictures, especially in colour, an important element if the ad must be visually striking. Magazines are also an excellent way to pass on coupons or even sample products. The biggest problem with magazines is their "lead" time — ad spaces usually need to be reserved months before actual publication. Magazines also take a long time to reach their total audience since each person will probably spend a few days reading it. This will be a problem if the company you're advertising for is having a two-day only sale!

NEWSPAPERS: News is read daily "hot off the press". Unlike magazines, newspapers cover their total audience in a very short space of time. Many readers actually use the newspapers as a means of getting more information about sales promotions, making it an action medium. Newspapers also

A TENNIS RACQUET TO PROMOTE THE LE VISION. GREAT VISUAL IDEAS DO NOT AGINATION. DENTSU YOUNG & RUBICAM SINGAPORE

offer short "lead" times and impressive penetrations into local markets. This comes at a high price with full-page ad spaces sometimes running into tens of thousands of dollars.

IF YOU LOVE NUMBER CRUNCHING...

As you have seen, the media department's job is an extremely important one in deciding the direction of a campaign. But how do they crunch their numbers anyway? Let's look at this now. In simple terms, the efficiency of each medium can be understood by looking at their reach and frequency. Reach refers to the percentage of target audience that has been exposed to the ad over a given period, usually taken to be four weeks. Frequency, on the other hand, refers to the number of times the target audience is exposed to the ad over the same period. These two pieces of data are interrelated. Assuming a fixed advertising budget, an increase in reach will result in lower frequency and vice versa. Let's illustrate this with a simple example. First, let's assume that we have ten programmes into which we can slot an ad, and each programme has one viewer. Placing an ad in all ten will allow ten viewers to see the ad once, giving us maximum reach. However, by redistributing the same ten ads over just five of the time slots, although only five people get to see the ads, they will see it twice. Since any advertising campaign has monetary limitations, the media department has to decide whether reach or frequency is more important. For example, the launch of a new product would require a greater reach to create increased awareness among consumers.

HEY, YOU CAN ALWAYS BE THE CLIENT

To find a career in advertising, you don't always have to look towards the advertising agency. The client organisations offer plenty of opportunities for aspiring young marketers. Highly professional marketing operators like Procter and Gamble,

Nestlé and Unilever offer traditional career paths: starting as a product executive, then product manager, rising up to brand manager, marketing manager and marketing director. These multinationals, many of which are in the fast-moving consumer goods business, offer excellent training and guidance for the totally inexperienced.

As a product executive, your job will revolve around a particular product or product line and its marketing, sales and sometimes even production aspects. You will be supporting the product management, and at the same time learning all about the product in relation to its marketing. While the job itself is not totally about advertising, there will be opportunities to work with the advertising agency in developing thematic and tactical advertisements. The job offers new marketers an excellent way of gaining an overall perspective of how products are marketed.

Many firms also have a marketing or an A & P (advertising and promotions) department either in support or in place of product management teams. Companies in finance (e.g. Citibank, American Express) or service industries (e.g. Hyatt Hotels & Resorts, Qantas Airways) all depend on such departments to handle advertising and communication tasks. In such departments, a typical entry position will be a marketing executive supporting an advertising manager or corporate communications director, reporting to or working in co-operation with a marketing director.

Some other possible job titles would include A & P manager, promotions manager and even sales manager. How these positions relate to one another is usually unique to each company and industry. Working in the A & P department, young executives will be involved in the execution of A & P plans, both internal (within the firm) and external. They will get to work as partners with the agency, research firms and other suppliers.

64
SOME CLIENTS OWN THEIR OWN AGENCIES...

And it's not a new development. One famous ad agency name – Lintas – was originally an acronym for Lever International Advertising Service.

Today, many advertising agency services have been "unbundled". The agency is no longer seen as the single source for strategic, creative and media services. Some clients like Benetton do their own creative work. At one stage, Coca-Cola sought ideas from many different agencies and even went direct to Hollywood for television concepts and production. One major watch company buys its creative and media from independent, unbundled sources. In New York, Avon Products, Inc. has an in-house creative agency with a staff of over 500, as well as using mainstream advertising agencies.

BOWING TO PUBLIC PRESSURE, RAFFLES HOTEL OPENS A SINGLES BAR.

Which immediately presents us with two problems.
The first problem first: Young men, eager to cohabit with lithe members of the
opposite sex are not encouraged to invade the Bar & Billiard Room.

(Well, having said that, let us hasten to add they are most welcome to attempt enjoyment of the prime purpose of this advertisement.)

Which raises the second problem: We are offering you tonight an unbridled opportunity to explore some of Scotland's finest achievements.

means that the youngest of the whiskies has been aged for at least 12 years, whilst the others are anyone's guess, laddie.

Whereas a 12-year old single malt whisky is purely and precisely that: one grand old whisky in all its majestic and undiluted glory.

distiller's art itself. The subtle aromas and flavours have never been quite fully explained, possibly because no one is sufficiently sober afterwards.

THE FACT THAT a proud single malt calls to mind the misty glens, heather-blanketed hillsides, crystal streams teeming with trout, skirling pipes, etcetera, should also call to mind one other minuscule detail: *the price*.

Rest assured, with all their true canny, the Scots will endeavour to extract as much money from your pocket as they can in exchange for their best single malts. And who's to blame them?

The most noble array of single malt Scotch Whisky, this side of Skye.

However, there is a prevailing view that a single malt whisky is but another manifestation of the Scottish national trait: reluctance to part with things of value.

Like money.

Or whisky.

Sadly, many a novice Scotch drinker is convinced that a single malt whisky will not deliver his money's worth, whereas a bottle containing several malt whiskies will.

Ah, clever people the Scots. For nothing could be further from the truth.

THE TRUTH IS, a blend is merely a blend. Read our lips: A 12-year old blended whisky

HAVING GRASPED THAT inescapable fact, you may think the rest is easy. Not so, for the Scots are full of contradictions.

As if foreseeing the day when our Bar & Billiard Room would voraciously pry sizeable quantities of their precious single malt whiskies from their homeland, the Scots set about giving them virtually unpronounceable names.

Glenfiddich, Glenmorangie, Dalwhinnie, Auchentoshan, Bladnoch and Laphroaig. A fiendish deterrent, indeed, but one which can be simply overcome by the use of our single malt whisky guide and an index finger.

One final hurdle remains.

Unravelling the mysteries of classic single and rare malt whiskies is as daunting as the

OF COURSE, OUR Bar & Billiard Room offers many other aristocratic distractions.

A Krug, the Grande Cuvee predictably.

Or La Grande Dame 1985, secured at no little expense from the House of Veuve Clicquot.

Or an amber Belle Vue Gueuze from Belgium's master brewers.

Not forgetting the most fastidious array of fine armagnacs, cognacs, ports, coffees and Valrhona chocolates ever to be savoured over a lazy game of billiards.

SUCH IS THE Bar & Billiard Room. If not a singles bar, by every means a singular bar. And a haven which awaits you after work, after dinner or after the theatre, tonight and every night.

GETT

CLUE No. 3:

NG UP

TO SPEED

What is happening in the advertising business today? What kind of changes are likely to happen this year, next year, and five years from now?

Because advertising is changing so quickly, can you still plan on having an advertising career?

HOW IS
ADVERTISING
CHANGING?

More often than not, today's advertisers don't need a full-service agency. They pick and choose the services they want. And they negotiate different fees for the services they buy. Today, the marketing communications menu looks something like this:

ABOVE-THE-LINE is the term for mainstream paid advertising in newspapers, magazines, television, radio, transit ads and outdoor posters.

BELOW-THE-LINE. In addition to mainstream advertising, the advertising agency or a specialist company develops and co-ordinates other forms of promotions. Sales promotion and merchandising work together with advertising to form a complete promotional campaign. The areas that these two activities cover can be considered to be everything that doesn't involve the communication of product information through paid media. Non-paid media can even include sponsorships of sports stars and live telecasts. Although advertising can bring awareness of a product to the consumer, sales promotions are what gets the products into the shops in the first place. Merchandising then helps to not just make the consumer buy the product, but keeps the consumer's loyalty after that first purchase as well. Sales promotions and merchandising are both means to motivate and inform not only the consumer, but the entire sales and distribution network.

SALES PROMOTION, which goes out to retailers as well as consumers, usually starts way before any advertising campaign. For example, before any campaign commences, the distributors have to be convinced to first stock up on the new product. This is not an easy task, since the distributor has to commit money, inventory space, or even sacrifice another product line in order to make way for the new one. To achieve this objective, the company first has to inform and motivate their internal sales team. A sales team that knows what it is selling will be able to add more punch to their sales pitch. The team needs to be briefed with sales kits and training on the new product's specifications, and the advantages it has over the competitors' products. These kits can include visual aids like promotional videos and catalogues. Extra motivation can also come from sales-incentive programmes. Once the sales team is informed and motivated, they'll be better positioned to sell to the distributors. The same training and sales kits presented to the company's sales team must also be made available to the distributor. Catalogues, price lists and video demonstrations will help them sell into retail outlets. But it doesn't stop there.

MERCHANDISING is the most direct contact the advertiser can have with the consumer. Once the product gets into retail outlets, merchandising takes over a huge part of the campaign. It's the war at retail level! Retail outlets — the point of sale — will have to be provided with posters, signage displays, window banners, floor stickers, shelf "talkers" and even bumper stickers. Sometimes the product can be "sampled" in supermarkets. Promotions involving gifts and prizes can also be staged in retail outlets or shopping malls, often by radio and TV stars. Merchandising could well be the nudge that pulls a customer away from a competing brand at the point of purchase. Because merchandising makes use of detailed information on who buys what in order to target each individual consumer, direct mail with discount coupons or free trial offers can be sent to the consumers themselves to raise awareness. (Care is taken that mailings go out to consumers from a list of names and addresses that best represents potential buyers or users.) Another channel would be telemarketing, where products are demonstrated on TV and consumers can call a number to make a purchase. All these activities are considered part of merchandising, and help to push forward the sales promotion campaign by once again informing and motivating consumers. It is important that the sales promotion, merchandising and advertising campaign all run along the same theme in order to produce the greatest communicative power to the consumer. Any incongruity may just leave a disorientated consumer who probably won't buy a product from a company that can't even co-ordinate its sales campaign.

CUSTOMER RELATIONS MARKETING. With such fierce competition in today's marketplace, customer relations marketing (once known as after-sales service) is gaining importance. Loyalty programmes are almost the rule in some categories. Airlines offer frequent flyer miles as a customer reward to build long-term loyalty. Petrol companies offer free gifts based on frequent repeat purchases. Take an example of a bank's credit card system to see how a sale is first achieved and then customer loyalty maintained using information technology. If a bank has decided to launch a credit card, it can first get a list of new graduates and send them a brochure. Not only is this a targeted sales promotion, it could even be personalised with a "for you" only special, like "0% interest for the first year" if you apply within a certain time period. Assuming that this person signs on, the sales promotion does not just end there. Close monitoring of this person's spending habits can allow the bank to increase the number of services it can provide. For example, if this person starts buying furniture, this could be indicative of the buying of a new home, prompting the bank to send brochures for a home loan. The purchase from children's retail outlets may spur the bank to send life insurance policy brochures. Spending habits can be used to preempt the customer by providing many services at the right time. Such personalised forms of merchandising aim to prevent the customer from considering other banks, and encourage loyalty.

THROUGH-THE-LINE is the term describing campaigns that combine paid above-the-line media and below-the-line activities. Many people believe that this holistic approach will become the future of advertising because advertisers can no longer rely on mass media advertising alone.

DARK, SATIRICAL HUMOUR CREATED THE MOOD FOR MARTELL EXILE. THE USE OF NURSERY RHYMES GAVE THE CAMPAIGN AN EXTRA TWIST OF IRONY.
DENTSU YOUNG & RUBICAM SINGAPORE

HOW ARE AGENCIES CHANGING?

Advertising is evolving faster now than ever before. Traditional agency structures with formal departments are being challenged by new agencies without walls. Agency services are being unbundled and dozens of small, independent creative boutiques are springing up to offer direct marketing, design and promotions.

How do new cutting edge agencies operate?

GROUND ZERO, SANTA MONICA. The agency calls itself a "community". Brand teams contain strategic, creative and media people working together, and clients are encouraged to move into the agency. Founding partner Kirk Souder, one of America's most admired young creatives, believes a company should exist for its people. "When people come to Ground Zero, both clients and employees alike, we ask them to be selfish with their time here. We ask them to look at every task as an opportunity to fulfil their own personal growth, their own personal journey to the truth, and to try what they've never tried before." If people do that, says Souder, the work will feel fresh, innovative and important — and so will the people doing it.

HOWELL HENRY CHALDECOTT LURY, LONDON. The agency describes itself as "Professional Radicals". Instead of having different departments, people from each discipline work in teams — a typical project team would comprise an account director, a planner, a writer and an art director. Each close-knit team is like a SWAT unit; it lives and breathes its account, and everybody has a share in creating the work. HHCL has created some of Britain's most electrifying work like the Tango *Orange Man*, First Direct Bank, and Maxell. Steve Henry says that when the agency started, all the partners with their different skills sat together in one room. "As we grew and hired more people, we could have gone the conventional way and split up into different departments. But we wanted to preserve the magic, the chemistry, that happened when you mixed the different disciplines together."

SPRINGER & JACOBY, HAMBURG. Germany's most creative agency, with major accounts like Mercedes-Benz, reinvented itself several years ago. It wanted to offer clients a more flexible, multi-cultured environment. It hived itself off into six independent agency units located within a 500-metre radius of each other. Each unit operates autonomously; it is free to work on its own style of advertising, with its own totally different working process. When it needs support (for example, with media, research or planning) it calls on departments at the central core agency. Clients enjoy working directly with smaller units, and having access to the key people on their accounts. And should clients want a change, they can move to a different unit within the agency — without actually changing agency.

ST. LUKE'S, LONDON. When Chiat/Day London was about to be merged into TBWA, Andy Law drew a line across the floor and asked his staff to step over it if they wanted to take a gamble on starting a new agency with him. Everyone crossed the line. He set up a trust to buy the agency back for two million pounds. Three years later, St. Luke's was hailed Britain's Agency of the Year. No one has a desk, only a locker. Clients have Brand Rooms. The agency produces cutting edge work but never enters award shows. An artist-in-residence has decked out the agency as a church and a hospital. When someone applies for a job they are asked how they will change the company. After six months, everyone is given shares in the company and after five years they can enjoy paid sabbatical leave.

Black-and-white images in slow motion flow to traditional Chinese music. There is no voice-over.

A woman slowly pulls a barrow piled high with vegetables through frame.

SUPER *Someone else's child will supply food for your family.*

Dissolve to a road building crew at work.

SUPER *Someone else's child will pave the road you walk on.*

Dissolve to a taxi driving along a Chinese street, trees reflected in its windscreen.

SUPER *Someone else's child will take you to work every day.*

Dissolve to a policeman apprehending a thief in an alley.

SUPER *Someone else's child will protect you from danger.*

Dissolve to an ambulance arriving at a hospital gate and nurses rushing to open its doors.

SUPER *Some one else's child will save your life.*

Dissolve to soldiers riding in an army truck.

SUPER *Someone else's child is even prepared to die for you.*

Dissolve to a teacher writing on a blackboard and her class putting up their hands.

SUPER *All they need is a chance… to grow up like yours.*

Dissolve to UNICEF logo with slogan: *Ér tóng zhī yǒu. (Children's friend.)*

A CHINESE PUBLIC SERVICE COMMERCIAL CREATED BY SAATCHI & SAATCHI BEIJING TO SHOW UNICEF'S WORK IN A NEW PERSPECTIVE. BEAUTIFULLY FILMED IN BLACK AND WHITE, IT COMMUNICATED THAT WE ARE ALL DEPENDENT ON "SOMEONE ELSE'S CHILD", INCLUDING THE CHILDREN THAT UNICEF HELPS.

WHAT DOES IT ALL MEAN?

Advertising people seem to speak a quaint foreign language. Here it is decoded:

A

4As Most countries have a collective industry association that represents the interests of all advertising agencies. Often called the 4As (The Association of Accredited Advertising Agents), it will set rules and fees which its members agree to follow. America, Hong Kong and Singapore use the term 4As; in Australia, it's called the AFA (Advertising Federation of Australia), and in Britain, the IPA (Institute of Practitioners in Advertising).

AMBIENT MEDIA These days advertisers are taking consumers by surprise, implanting advertising messages in unexpected places like pavements, or on the sides of buildings. One agency in New Zealand had red dye gurgling away in a fountain to promote a horror movie on TV.

ANIMATIC A way of demonstrating how a commercial concept will look when completed. Illustrations, still photographs or film footage are edited to a soundtrack and presented to advertisers and research groups on videotape.

AUDIO The sound track of a TV commercial.

AMBIENT MEDIA CATCHES THE CONSUMER BY SURPRISE. OGILVYONE WORLDWIDE HONG KONG CHOSE WALLS, COLUMNS, BUSES AND AIRPORT TROLLEYS TO COMMUNICATE MESSAGES FOR *THE ECONOMIST*. BY USING THE SAME RED AND WHITE AS THE MAGAZINE'S MASTHEAD, THE ADS REINFORCED THE BRAND IMAGE.

B/W A black and white print ad that uses no colour. Also referred to as a **mono** (monochrome) ad.

BALLOONS In comic strips, the words of dialogue are contained in a circle called a "balloon" or a "speech balloon". When balloons are given jagged edges in advertising, they are called "bomb bursts" and usually contain prices or urgent messages like "Save 30%" or "Hurry, Last Days".

BILLINGS The term used to describe the total amount of money spent by a client through the agency. Some accounts "bill" thousands of dollars, others "bill" millions.

BLEED A bleed page in a magazine is when the advertisement extends to the four edges of the page so there is no white border.

CDP Collett Dickenson Pearce is a legendary British agency famous for outstanding creative work in the 1970s and 1980s. Its work is still used as a reference for creative standards today.

CIA Not the spy organisation, but a media consultancy (Chris Ingram Associates) originally founded in Britain and now part of WPP.

CIRCULATION The number of copies sold or distributed per issue of a publication.

COLOUR SEPARATIONS The stage of four-colour printing when each separate colour film can be checked individually in a set of "colour seps".

COLUMNS Newspaper and magazine pages are divided into vertical columns. Ad sizes and costs in newspapers are expressed in column centimetres — for example, a 28 x 5 is an advertisement measuring 28 centimetres deep by 5 columns wide.

CONSUMER The present or potential buyer of a brand, product or service.

COPY The text of a print ad, or the script of a TV or radio commercial. A *copy test* is a research process that aims to assess consumer reactions to the ad.

COST-PER-THOUSAND (CPM) The cost to the advertiser of reaching each 1,000 individuals or homes in the target audience.

D

D&AD British Design and Art Direction runs industry training programmes and the world's most prestigious award show.

DPS A double-page spread, with the advertisement running across the "gutter" between both pages. Great care has to be taken when producing a DPS so that the central letters of the headline don't disappear into the gutter when the magazine is bound.

DISPLAY ADS Print ads of a larger size using eye-catching visuals and typography to attract attention. Display ads are the opposite to classified ads.

EXPOSURE

A PERSON'S PHYSICAL CONTACT WITH AN ADVERTISING MEDIUM OR MESSAGE.

F

FPC A full page, full colour print advertisement. If only one colour is used, it is often called a spot colour ad or a second colour ad.

FACE Each group or family of type designs is called a typeface. Popular faces include Futura, Garamond, Gill Sans, Helvetica and Times.

GRPs

GROSS RATING POINTS. CONFUSED? KEEP READING!

I

INITIAL CAPS Sometimes You Will See Headlines Set In Lower Case, Where The First Letter Of Each Word Has Been Capitalised For Artistic Effect. Hard To Read, Isn't It?

INTERPUBLIC The first big agency holding company started in 1960 by McCann-Erickson.

L

LANDSCAPE A horizontally-formatted print ad where the width is greater than the depth.

LAYOUT The plan of how a print advertisement will look when it is finished. These days layouts are usually created on an Apple Mac using "scrap" art collected from books and magazines, although some art directors prefer to keep them rough (hand-lettered and hand-drawn) and not too highly finished. Layouts are used to present print ideas to clients.

M

MVO Male Voice-Over in a TV script. No prizes for guessing what FVOs are.

MASTHEAD The distinctive front page design of a newspaper's title, or the front cover design of a magazine's title.

O

OMNICON A huge conglomerate comprising agencies like BBDO, DDB and Needham Harper.

OTS Opportunities-to-see are the number of times the target audience will be exposed to the TV channel screening the commercial.

M&C SAATCHI SINGAPORE USED CHINESE PAINTINGS TO COMMUNICATE HOW THE NEW BMW X5 OFF-ROAD VEHICLE WOULD GO ANYWHERE.

P

POP OR POS Point of Purchase or Point of Sale.

PITCH Nothing to do with music. A pitch is when an agency tenders for new business — the agency team "pitches" its ideas across the table to a panel of client executives. Some cynics believe body language is just as important as what the agency is presenting.

POST-PRO Short for post-production, the final stage of a TV commercial's execution when it is colour-graded and edited, and music and voice-over are added.

PREMIUM A free or specially-reduced item offered to consumers as an inducement to buy a product or use a service.

PRINT RUN The number of copies printed in one "run" of the presses. Some newspapers have print runs of 400,000 copies.

PROOFS

GALLEY PROOFS, PAGE PROOFS, PROGRESSIVE PROOFS, COLOUR PROOFS AND MACHINE PROOFS ARE JUST SOME OF THE QUALITY CONTROL STAGES IN PRODUCING BROCHURES, CATALOGUES, ANNUAL REPORTS AND POSTERS.

R

RATING POINTS A rating point equals one percent of the target audience universe. **Gross Rating Points (GRPs)** are a measure of the total ad weight delivered by the campaign — the sum total of ratings for each individual ad exposure.

REACH AND FREQUENCY Reach is the percentage of target audience exposed to the client's message during a designated period (usually four weeks). **Frequency** refers to the average number of times within that period that those reached are exposed to the ad.

READERSHIP The total number of individuals reading a publication. For example, a magazine might have a **circulation** of 200,000, but if each copy is read on average by three people then its **readership** will be 600,000.

RECALL Measures consumer memorability of an ad or commercial. Recall tests can be aided or unaided.

RESPONDENTS Consumers interviewed in research.

RESPONSE The number of consumers who respond to a particular promotional activity.

REVERSE TYPE A reverse headline means it will appear white on black, or in a contrasting colour over a photograph or illustration. Many experts believe that headlines are easiest to read when the lettering is black, rather than being "reversed" out of another colour.

RUN OF PRESS, RUN OF PAPER Print ads that are placed at standard rates anywhere in a publication. If the advertiser buys a fixed position, he will usually pay a "loading" or premium to obtain his **preferred position**.

S

SCAMP A rough hand-drawn layout of a print ad.

SCREEN The number of dots printed per square inch. A 65-screen ad will look very coarse compared to a 120-screen ad.

SCRAP ART Photographs or illustrations torn from magazines and used in layouts to demonstrate how the finished ad will look.

SERIF AND SANSERIF A serif is a small terminal stroke at the end of the main stroke of a letter. Times is a serif typeface, Helvetica is sanserif. Generally, serif typefaces are easier to read, which is why most of the text in newspapers and books is set in serif faces. However, headlines are set in either serif or sanserif typefaces, depending on taste and the effect required.

SOV Share of Voice is the percentage of your ad budget within the total ad spending in your product category. Leo Burnett once said, "Before you can have a share of market, you must have a share of mind."

STORYBOARD A storyboard looks like a big comic strip. Every scene of a TV commercial is drawn in colour, with the soundtrack printed beneath, to help clients visualise the way the message will be presented.

24-SHEET POSTER Outdoor poster sizes are expressed in the number of pieces of paper needed to cover the panel. Other popular sizes are 12-sheet and 10-sheet posters.

T

TARPS Target Audience Rating Points.

TEAR SHEETS The page containing an advertisement is "torn" from the magazine as proof that it actually appeared. Media invoices to clients have tear sheets attached to substantiate that the ads appeared in accordance with the schedule.

TRANSIT Transit media include bus ads, taxi tops and posters at bus stops and rail stations.

U

UPPER CASE Headlines or body copy set in CAPITAL LETTERS. Many experts believe that headlines set in lower case are easier to read THAN THOSE SET IN CAPS.

W

WPP Martin Sorrell's Wire & Paper Products owns and operates many famous agencies like JWT, O&M and Batey Ads.

WIDOWS When a paragraph of copy ends with one word on a line by itself, the space created is called a widow. While widows are generally avoided by resetting the text or adding extra words, the occasional short line helps let "air" into the text and makes it more inviting to read.

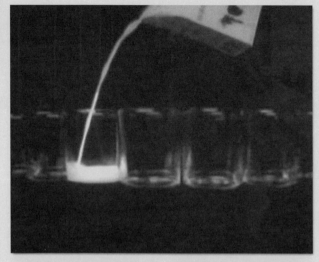

Eight empty glasses are lined up against a black backdrop. Milk is poured into three of them and we begin to see that the glasses have been arranged like a row of teeth.

The other glasses are left empty, conveying the impression of missing teeth.

MVO *These are your kids' teeth if they don't get enough calcium.*

The remaining glasses are now filled so they replicate a row of perfectly healthy teeth.

MVO *For stronger teeth, drink more milk.*

END PACK SHOT Nong Pho High Calcium Milk.

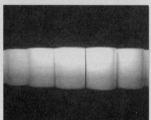

BBDO BANGKOK CREATED THE NONG PHO MILK TV COMMERCIAL.

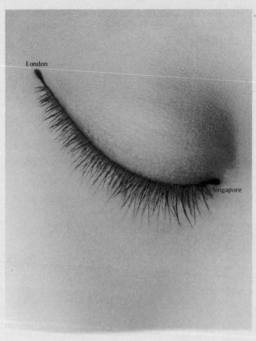

London

Singapore

FIRST
BRITISH AIRWAYS
The world's favourite airline

M&C SAATCHI SINGAPORE COMMUNICATED A NEW FIRST CLASS SLEEPER BED FOR BRITISH AIRWAYS USING ONE PHOTO AND TWO WORDS.

ADVERTISING AWARDS: AND THE WINNER IS...

Winning creative awards helps an agency boost its stature in the industry and attract better creative people. The publicity from winning awards often brings it to the attention of advertisers shopping around for a new agency.

Winning awards is almost essential to build a creative career. Recognition at an early age has propelled many young agency creatives into positions of power before they turned 30.

Some awards are easier to win than others. Some awards carry little or no respect at all. The three toughest, most important, most respected award shows in the world are:

D&AD

REGARDED BY MOST CREATIVES AS THE WORLD'S TOP AWARD SHOW, IT IS JUDGED BY BRITISH JURIES AND ATTRACTS 20,000 ENTRIES A YEAR IN ADVERTISING AND DESIGN CATEGORIES. A GOLD PENCIL, WHICH IS ACTUALLY BLACK, AND A SILVER PENCIL, WHICH IS ACTUALLY YELLOW, ARE VERY HARD TO WIN. FEW GOLDS HAVE EVER BEEN WON OVER THE YEARS. EVEN BEING NOMINATED FOR A SILVER, OR BEING A FINALIST, IS AN HONOUR THAT ONLY A HANDFUL OF CREATIVES WILL ACHIEVE EACH YEAR. EVERY YOUNG CREATIVE SHOULD INVEST IN A COPY OF THE D&AD ANNUAL.

THE ONE SHOW is America's top award show, conducted by New York's The One Club for Art and Copy. Like D&AD, The One Club is a non-profit industry organisation that upholds creative standards and helps train young talent. Awards are Gold, Silver and Bronze, judged mostly by American juries. The One Show is also fiercely contested by British and Asian agencies. Winners and finalists are celebrated in a glossy colour annual that every young creative should buy.

THE INTERNATIONAL ADVERTISING FESTIVAL at Cannes awards Gold, Silver and Bronze Lions. The judging panels are drawn from all over the world, and the awards ceremony every June climaxes a week of creative seminars attended by thousands of elite advertising professionals. Some countries that do very well at Cannes include Brazil, Japan, Scandinavia, Singapore and Spain.

A fourth annual that is regarded highly in America is **CA (Communications Arts)** — it attracts well over 10,000 entries, but the annual is barely half an inch thick!

Other popular award shows include the **Art Directors Club of New York**, **CLIO**, **London International Advertising Awards**, **Mobius**, and the **New York Festivals**.

Many creative directors will only enter award shows that produce an annual. Without a book that provides a permanent historic record, they believe that people will soon forget the winners and their work.

Regional and local award shows are an important arena for young creatives to first gain recognition. The **Asian Advertising Awards** is conducted in Hong Kong by *Media* magazine. **Adfest** in Thailand is contested every March, and **AWARD** Australia provides a showcase for Asian, Australian and New Zealand agencies to do creative battle.

Each Asian country has its own annual awards show, some judged by a local panel entirely, others by a mix of local and foreign judges. Singapore has the **Creative Circle Awards**, Malaysia has the **Kancil Awards**, Thailand has the **BAD Awards** (BAD stands for Bangkok Art Directors) and Hong Kong has the **Kam Fan Awards**.

For perfect teeth, see your dentist.

SINGAPORE DENTAL ASSOCIATION

A VISUALLY-LED AD HAS THE IDEA IN THE PICTURE. THIS IS HOW BBDO BANGKOK COMMUNICATED PIZZA HUT'S NEW ONLINE PIZZA SERVICE.

Being "Larry", the last crayfish in the tank of a Chinese seafood restaurant, is about as stressful as it gets.

As the commercial unfolds, the crayfish darts behind a rock whenever a Chinese employee emerges from the kitchen or passes the tank. We hear the Chinese restaurant ambience as Larry might hear it — an alien, threatening hubbub beyond the glass. Larry's agitated underwater scuttling noises add to the tension.

Just when Larry finally retreats behind a rock, a super establishes the subject matter: *Living with stress?*

Cut to the product and end super.

FVO *Executive B Stress Formula with Herbs from Blackmores. The best of health.*

A SIMPLE, HUMOROUS TREATMENT OF A STRESSFUL SUBJECT, BY SYDNEY AGENCY BROWN MELHUISH FISHLOCK.

HOW CA

CLUE No. 4:
PAIGNS
ARE MADE

Every advertising campaign is the work of many people, not just creative people. It all begins with the client, who identifies a need for advertising. He will call his agency and "brief" the account service executives. They, in turn, have to "brief' the creative department.

SHAPING THE STRATEGY

The first and most important aspect of the advertising strategy is the goal, and it should be the first thing that you put down. The goal depends on what the client wants to achieve, and you would normally repeat the sales goal and marketing objective. If you wish to increase profit margin, your goals would be fiscal in nature, while volume goals can be stated for sale items. Then you would add on an advertising objective. Awareness goals could involve the launch of a new product and the need to publicise it. Attitudinal-change goals are needed if you're about to reshape your company's image. But lofty aims won't do without a practical plan, so you'll also need to be guided by a reasonable marketing strategy and a budget that can aid in achieving the ad objectives.

After you're done with the goals, move on to the battle plans. These will need to detail what advertising can do to achieve stated objectives. First, you'll need to define the target market. You should define the primary and secondary groups in detail. Put down all the information on the target audience's demographics, as well as geographic and seasonal information. Basically your strategy should match the target audiences' needs with a proposed positioning. Define what your competitors are doing and their positioning. Past ad copies would be useful in determining the tactics being used by competitors and their activities.

Next in your strategy should come the proposed basis of advertising. It essentially directs what the advertisement is supposed to achieve. Some agencies use before and after format as in "What the target audience thinks of my product now" and "How I want them to see my product after the campaign". Others prefer just a short but powerful statement, no longer than one, single-minded sentence. Think through clearly why a particular proposition can be the solution to a problem. If research has been utilised, you'll also need to list down findings from a market test of your proposal. State your proposed positioning in clear and succinct terms. Finally, include the estimated budget to achieve the task at hand, and any mandatories like logos and font types.

GETTING BRIEFED

The conceptualisation of a new campaign is always a crucial task. Creative sparks fly when there is sincere interest in the promotion of the product. The advertisers, through the account service department, must load the creative people with information and make them feel excited about the product; this is important because the agency may not have had much direct contact with the product.

Most clients have a template that lists the items to provide agencies. In reality a good brief for a full campaign should be a thorough package which includes:

1. PAST CAMPAIGNS

2. INTERNATIONAL CAMPAIGNS (IF ANY)

3. PRODUCT SAMPLES

4. MARKETING STRATEGY

5. SALES INFORMATION

6. CONSUMER RESEARCH DATA

7. COMPETITIVE INFORMATION

The more information the agency has at its fingertips, the more ammunition it will have in developing the big idea.

The advertisers must give enough freedom to the creative team, and yet limit their expressions within a fixed scope. However, many advertisers tend to kill the most innovative ideas at an early stage by rejecting them as not being what they had envisioned. Or, they may not be fixed on their objectives and continually shift directions. This may not only kill excellent ideas, but will also frustrate the creative team. This frustration will kill any enthusiasm that the team has, leading to less unique ideas. The agency on the other hand should never stop disagreeing with the advertisers. If they simply adopt the strategy that the advertisers have proposed, the final product will probably not be as good as what it could have been. (In agencies, this is called "take the money and run".)

In many agencies, the brief will not proceed to the creative teams until the creative director has accepted it. Writers and art directors work within a certain creative framework. If the brief does not fit that framework, it is returned. The best briefs will have simplified the problem to a one-word or one-sentence proposition. The proposition is the single promise that the advertising will make to the target audience. It might be "refreshment" or "strength".

The best account service people and planners are the ones who work like detectives — digging deeper and deeper until they find something really unique to say, or a way to show the product in a new light. Famous British adman Robin Wight called this "interrogating the product until it confesses its strengths". Lazy account service people take the easy way out. For example, they might say that "friendly service" is the proposition for a bank. An experienced creative director would throw it back as being "generic"; all banks claim to be friendly, so what? Creative minds will be looking for a unique twist or hook, for something to talk about in the advertising that nobody else has said before. Some briefs will even have ideas in them.

FIVE STEPS TO AD STRATEGY
1.SPECIFY THE KEY FACT:
A single-minded statement from the customer's points of view that identifies why consumers are or are not purchasing the brand.

2.STATE THE MARKETING PROBLEM:
States the problem from the marketer's point of view.

3.STATE THE COMMUNICATIONS OBJECTIVE:
What effect the advertising is intended to have on the target market and how it should persuade consumers.

4.IMPLEMENT THE CREATIVE MESSAGE STRATEGY
5.ESTABLISH MANDATORY CORPORATE/DIVISIONAL REQUIREMENTS

CREATIVE STRATEGY IN PRACTICE

1. OBJECTIVE
2. TARGET AUDIENCE
3. POSITIONING
4. PROPOSITION
5. SUPPORT
6. TONE AND MANNER
7. MANDATORIES

CREATIVE STRATEGIES DEFINED BY
THE ADVERTISING GREATS

DAVID OGILVY'S BRAND IMAGE

- Consumers buy physical, psychological benefits, not products.
- Advertising should be a long-term investment in the development and retention of a brand image.

LEO BURNETT'S INHERENT DRAMA

- Find the drama in a product.
- Identify the reason why the manufacturer makes the product.
- Identify the reason the consumer purchases the product.

ROSSER REEVES' (TED BATES AGENCY) U.S.P.

- Each ad must make a proposition.
- The proposition must be the one that the competition cannot and does not offer.
- The proposition must be strong enough to attract new customers.

WHAT IS A UNIQUE SELLING
PROPOSITION (U.S.P.)?

SUPERIORITY CLAIMS BASED ON UNIQUE PHYSICAL FEATURE OR BENEFIT.

The airline with the most modern fleet in the world, still believes in the romance of travel.

Fly with us to four continents in the comfort of the world's most modern fleet, which includes exclusive 747 Super-8s and stretched upper deck 747s.   On the way, enjoy the kind of inflight service even other airlines talk about, with gentle hostesses in sarong kebayas caring for you as only they know how.

The airline with the most modern fleet in the world, still believes in the romance of travel.

Fly with us to four continents in the comfort of the world's most modern fleet, which includes exclusive 747 Super-8s and stretched upper deck 747s.   On the way, enjoy the kind of inflight service even other airlines talk about, with gentle hostesses in sarong kebayas caring for you as only they know how.

A CAMPAIGN WELL WORTH STUDYING: THE SINGAPORE GIRL FROM BATEY ADS SINGAPORE.

WHAT IS A GOOD BRIEF?

The brief is the springboard for the creative work. It should be the single starting point for the creative process. And it should identify the central thing that the ads have to communicate. But if the client, planner and account service executive simply follow the rules of the category, their brief will be a cookie-cutter replica of everyone else in the category. "The trouble with logic, process and analysis," warns Simon Sherwood of Bartle Bogle Hegarty, "is that everyone tends to end up in the same place."

British advertising legend Mike Cozens tells us that a factual brief is best, ending with a single-minded, single-worded proposition. The proposition should be based on product differentiation.

America's Ron Lawner of Arnold Communications, Boston, wants a brief to tell him what niche the product occupies, what the issues are in the category, and what the consumers are thinking. He says you must have a clear idea of the consumers' mindset and where the product might fit into their lives. "Demographics don't buy things, people do…"

"Most great ideas come from the brief," says Neil French, Worldwide Creative Director of Ogilvy & Mather.

So, the better the brief, the better the creative will be.

CREATIVE STAGES
1. PREPARE
2. INCUBATE
3. ILLUMINATE
4. VERIFY

WHAT IS
ADVERTISING
CREATIVITY?

The most precious commodity in advertising is a "big enduring idea", something all agency creatives strive to produce. By this we refer to the creative solution to address the marketing problem of the client, lasting over time to perhaps become classic marketing equity over the years. The search for the single, simple concept that will move people to buy is the true calling of creative people. In general, such an idea should:

1. **CREATE A HIGH LEVEL OF AWARENESS**
2. **CHANGE THE ATTITUDES OF THE TARGET AUDIENCE IN THE DIRECTION SET FORTH IN THE OBJECTIVES**
3. **BE FLEXIBLE ENOUGH FOR VARIATIONS IN MARKET CONDITIONS**
4. **BE EXECUTABLE WITH IMPACT IN MORE THAN ONE MEDIUM**
5. **BE ADAPTABLE ACROSS SALES PROMOTIONS, MERCHANDISING AND CUSTOMER RELATIONS MARKETING**

Creativity in an agency is not confined to the creative people, it exists in all areas of the agency in varying degrees. Aside from the creative department, those involved with creativity include the advertisers, the media and account people. Creativity needs to be bound tightly with marketing principles. For example, it is the advertiser's duty to spell out what they want, and the creative team to put together an ad that delivers the message in the most potent way. In that sense, good team management will lead to the most creative and effective ideas.

Advertisers and the creative personnel come together with very different backgrounds. Advertisers know their product inside out, and would probably have been dealing with the advertising campaign for months. The directions

AN EXAMPLE OF A TOTALLY INTEGRATED ADVERTISING CAMPAIGN: THE LAUNCH OF DOUBLE A PAPER, CREATED BY J. WALTER THOMPSON SINGAPORE. THE CONSUMER BENEFIT WAS THAT DOUBLE A PAPER WOULD NOT JAM IN PHOTOCOPIERS OR PRINTERS. THE CORE IDEA, *NO JAM*, WAS COMMUNICATED ON TV, PRINT ADS, TRANSIT POSTERS AND BUS ADS.

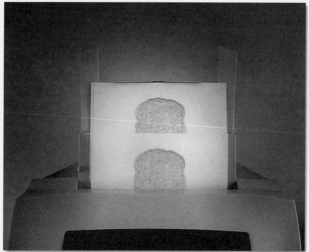

A steady stream of paper is emerging from a photocopier. Each page carries the picture of a plain slice of toast on it.

After a while the legend *No Jam* appears on the screen.

MVO Double A *paper is the smoothest paper to go into and come out of your photocopier.*

Pack shot appears on screen.

SUPER *Double A. Double Quality Paper.*

that the company has set for itself and its products may also restrict the amount of imaginative latitude the creatives can have. If a company projects a wholesome image, it would have guidelines for its advertising campaigns to be non-violent. The creative people on the other hand, are masters at communicating a product to an audience. Sometimes, they won't see eye to eye.

However, because the bottom line in advertising is to increase sales, an idea that wins awards may not necessarily achieve the objective. It is important for both sides to understand each group's professional boundary, and to keep certain objectives in mind at the conceptualisation stage.

GETTING
IDEAS

Once the brief is received there are many creative formulae for developing ideas. The best one is to turn off your computer. Computers don't have ideas; people do. And the best advertising ideas are always worked out with a pen and paper.

A good starting point is to look for ideas based on the product's name or its packaging or its heritage and history. Another good route for exploring ideas is to ask what might happen *with* the product and what might happen *without* it?

Many great creatives like Gary Goldsmith start with rational ideas and work "outwards" to intuitive ones. Goldsmith is very conscious of tone, too. The tone of an advertising idea, says Goldsmith, is "like a piece of clothing; it has got to fit the client. If it doesn't, they're not going to feel comfortable in it."

Fallon Minneapolis art director Dean Hanson describes many briefs as "laundry lists" of things the client and the account service executives would like to put in the ads. Isolating the key ideas is Hanson's critical first step. "I put down all the basic truths that I know. Then I try and put down in a sentence what it is we're trying to communicate. I'll put it up on the wall in its flattest, most mundane way; a sentence on the wall that says exactly what I'm going to say. And then I'll break it down. I'll think about the personality I want to project, the chemistry of the ad that I want, if it has to have dignity, if it has to be broad and humorous."

Neil French often finds inspiration from the product itself. It helps if the product is sitting on the table in front of him. The ads must not contradict the product, says French. "If you try to turn something nice and reliable into something frightfully hip and trendy, of course it doesn't work." French says if the product is going to be sold on a shelf, then put it on a shelf and look at it. Examine it from every angle, see how it reacts to light. Once he really knows the product, French puts it to one side and never looks at it again.

THE WAY AN AD IS ART DIRECTED IS THE WAY PEOPLE WILL READ IT

The eye enters the page at the top left corner, reads down, and leaves at the bottom right corner — and that's perhaps the most important thing to remember about art direction for newspaper and magazine ads. If the idea is in the picture, or the picture tells a visual joke, it should dominate the ad and the headline should follow below. If the idea for the ad is in the words, then the headline should come first and lead the reader into the picture.

COPYWRITERS BEWARE!

Some copywriters don't know when to stop copywriting! If the idea in the ad is visual, never follow it with a gimmicky headline. Let the picture do the work, and let the headline be a simple statement of fact or a simple promise. If both the words and the picture are funny or gimmicky, then one cancels out the other.

ART DIRECTORS BEWARE!

Some art directors don't know when to stop art directing! If the words have the idea — maybe they're saying something amusing, or they're asking an intriguing question — then the picture should be very simple and straightforward. The classic example was a Porsche ad created by Fallon Minneapolis. The idea was in the headline, which read: The fastest you can go without having to eat airline food. Directly below was a stock photo of a Porsche. (Art directors, please note also that there was no need to show a picture of airline food. If people reading the ad didn't know what airline food looked and tasted like, they wouldn't understand the headline anyhow.)

SELLING IDEAS
INSIDE THE AGENCY

Creative teams present their ideas to their creative group head or creative director. Usually one or two are chosen, improvements are made, and then the team (often with the creative director) will show them to the account service director and his team.

Very often a heated debate will follow, and the ideas will be rejected internally. Sometimes if no agreement can be reached on the work, a special agency review board meeting will be called to examine the whole project.

SELLING IDEAS
TO THE CLIENTS

Sometimes the agency's ideas are shown to the client at a formal "presentation". The account director or a senior team member will present the campaign's objectives and strategy, and the creative director will present the creative work, possibly with the copywriter and art director assisting.

Print ads are usually presented as colour printouts mounted on black or white card. Television is more difficult. It is almost impossible to convey the sense of a finished film without actually making it. Some agencies hold up drawn frames like a big comic strip, or produce video animatics complete with stock footage, music and graphics. Others prefer simply to stand up and read the scripts like a story, even putting on funny voices and acting out little scenes. They might also show a scene from a movie or a director's reel to help describe the kind of "look" or cinematographic treatment they have in mind for the finished commercial.

If you want guaranteed returns and the chance of a bonus, the only way is Up.

IDEALLY, THERE SHOULD BE SYNERGY IN A CAMPAIGN. IN THE TELEVISION COMMERCIAL FOR DBS BANK'S "UP", THE DOG'S EARS LIFTED UP. THE SAME VISUAL IDEA WAS CARRIED ACROSS TO PRINT ADS, POSTERS AND BROCHURES. TBWA SINGAPORE.

Now there's better way to grow your money. It's called Up. To find out more about Up, call Dial-n-Invest at **1800 222 7333** or visit any DBS Bank branch or DBS Securities. Alternatively, visit our website at www.dbs.com or www.DBSAM.com Up is also available at DBS Bank/POSB ATMs.

Up

⊠ DBS ASSET MANAGEMENT

⊠ DBS BANK

EVALUATING IDEAS

The creative team can usually only come up with good ideas when they actually feel for and share a bond with the product. With this in mind, the advertisers must also define the objectives of the campaign (whether it is to introduce a new product or defend it against a rival), the target audience, and list out its benefits to the consumer. After all, benefits to the "self" are what the consumer is most interested in, and ideas that can grab their self-interest will obviously be more effective in selling a product. It doesn't matter that an advertisement is really fantastic when the audience can only remember the ad and not the product — the so-called vampire effect.

Since different people have different aesthetic tastes, it is without doubt that there will be disagreements between the client and agency when the preliminary ideas have been delivered. This is where the consumer comes in. Focus groups and copy testing are intended to gauge consumer reactions before the advertising runs. The results of this research may point to a need to completely rework the campaign objectives. But the most radical of ideas should not be dropped hastily without proper reason or justification. There must be implicit trust present between both parties for this to work. This can be difficult since both sides believe that they have the last word on the advertisement — which means the process from conceptualisation to the final advertisement not only requires creative thinking, but tact in management as well.

EXECUTING
THE CAMPAIGN

Once the client has approved the work, it has to be "quoted". Usually three competitive quotes are obtained. The art buyer will call for quotes from the three photographers or illustrators best qualified to do the work. The broadcast department will call in three film companies; each will be briefed separately by the agency producer, copywriter and art director, and sometimes the creative director.

Frequently agencies will have made their choices long before the quotes come in. Some suppliers won't have been on the right "wavelength", while others will have made intelligent suggestions that add to the power of the idea. Many agency creative directors prefer to use film directors who have an agency background. They will be people who understand strategy, ideas and communication rather than being just people who can shoot pictures.

Once the client signs off on the financials, work begins. Clients are often invited to attend pre-production (or pre-pro) meetings at which casting, wardrobe and location decisions are made, and where the director will present his "shooting board" for approval. Some clients attend the actual shoot and insist on looking through the camera to check each shot before it is filmed.

Music and voice recording will usually take place at the post-production (or post-pro) stage. Editing will be completed in digital suites where images are often re-colourised and enhanced.

D'ARCY, MASIUS BENTON & BOWLES' UNIVERSAL ADVERTISING STANDARDS

- ❏ DOES THIS ADVERTISING POSITION THE PRODUCT SIMPLY AND WITH UNMISTAKABLE CLARITY?
- ❏ DOES THIS ADVERTISING BOLT THE BRAND TO A CLINCHING BENEFIT?
- ❏ DOES THIS ADVERTISING CONTAIN A POWER IDEA?
- ❏ DOES THIS ADVERTISING HAVE A DESIGNED-IN BRAND PERSONALITY?
- ❏ IS THIS ADVERTISING UNEXPECTED?
- ❏ IS THIS ADVERTISNG SINGLE-MINDED?
- ❏ DOES THIS ADVERTISING REWARD THE PROSPECT?
- ❏ IS THIS ADVERTISING VISUALLY ARRESTING?
- ❏ DOES THIS ADVERTISING EXHIBIT PAINSTAKING CRAFTSMANSHIP?

POINTERS FOR EFFECTIVE ADS

- ❏ MEETS STRATEGY
- ❏ ACHIEVES CONSUMER RESPONSE
- ❏ IS PERSUASIVE
- ❏ BREAKS THROUGH CLUTTER
- ❏ DELIVERS ON PROMISES
- ❏ DOESN'T OVERWHELM

ADVER

CLUE No. 5: I WANT TO WORK IN TISING

WHAT PREREQUISITES DO I NEED TO BE IN ADVERTISING?

First off, you should understand advertising, what it is, what it does and the processes involved. Once you have gained knowledge of advertising and the players involved in the business, you will have a good feel for which department would best suit you. For agency management, you need a good grounding in marketing. Most successful agency people have marketing sense that allows them to match a sales proposition with the commercial values of an idea. It is a bonus if you have a relevant degree (say, in marketing or advertising), but this is not a definite prerequisite. Many successful account people have non-relevant paper qualifications, but have learned the art of advertising well. This sense can be studied (by attending courses for example) and developed (from experience and observation).

I CAN'T DRAW. CAN I STILL BE IN ADVERTISING?

One of the most common questions asked by young people interested in advertising is, "I cannot even draw, so how could I be in such a creative industry?"

Although creativity entails the unhindered conceptualisation of ideas in the mind, it is not an anarchistic activity. In a sense, drawing can never really produce an entirely innovative creation, since it is only the expression of images that we have already stored in our memory. Instead, creativity flows from the way we express this imagery on paper — in both words and pictures.

So does the ability to draw have anything to do with creativity? It does, but drawing is more of a means to an end. In truth, "drawing" does not simply refer to the act of putting pencil to paper, but consists also of seeing and conceptualising. The process of representing thoughts either verbally or in written or pictorial form is important in advertising. Because we attempt to visualise things in pictures, drawing is merely the act of putting down these images. This process can take place on many fronts; through composition, colours and textures. The real bonus is being able to see things creatively, but being able to draw is not a prerequisite to work in an ad agency.

LEARN THE BUSINESS EVEN BEFORE YOU JOIN THE BUSINESS

Advertising trade publications can give you a quick pulse on the business. Even before you join it, you can read about the current issues and personalities, and get a deeper understanding of what is going on and what matters.

In Britain, *Campaign* is the weekly paper; in America, buy *Advertising Age* and *Adweek*. In Australia, buy *Adnews* and *B&T*.

In Asia, *Media* from Hong Kong has all the Asia-wide news, while Singapore's *AdAsia* and Malaysia's *ADOI* concentrate on South Asia.

For creatives, *Campaign Brief Australia* and *Campaign Brief Asia* give invaluable updates on new creative work, creative trends and interviews with the movers and shakers. Log onto **www.campaignbrief.com** to access the latest.

HOW TO INTERVIEW FOR AN ADVERTISING JOB

In every job application, it is seldom the most qualified person who gets the job. Rather, the successful person is the one most able to sell himself to the prospective employer. The interview is the part of the job application process where you'll have the chance to demonstrate your talents. So here are the steps that you should take before, during, and after an interview in order to secure that advertising job you seek.

Before you get an interview, first understand as much as you can about the advertising industry. Internships during school vacations are the best way to study the actual workplace and choose the area where you think your future might be.

First, get your résumé ready. Keep in mind that a company that has advertised a vacancy will receive hundreds of applications. Each letter only gets about a minute of reading time at most, so it is important that your résumé not be too long. Forget academic writing. Gerunds, verbs and an active voice will reflect a more dynamic personality. Phrases and fragments can help keep your résumé tight (using as few words as possible) and easy to read. Although you should not be self-effacing, you should also avoid the use of the egotistical sounding 'I'. While one page is ideal, two pages are about right in order not to sound too modest in putting down your attributes. Spell out everything that is related to the job that you're applying for, and what you have done that could be carried over to this position. Remember that the start and end of each paragraph are the most important, so keep the unimportant details in the middle. If you're a student, don't forget to list what you've learnt in your course of study; don't assume the course title is enough. Finally, state a time when you will contact the company to find out if you have been granted an interview. Leave the company you most want to work for until last. That way, you will have a chance to improve your interview technique and polish your résumé based on your other interview experiences.

You may wish to start off first with what is called an information interview. This is an interview with someone in the industry to get advice on entering the field. Once you get the interview, ask for job-hunting strategies and advice on your résumé. This will force the interviewer to look at it. If the interviewer is impressed, you may get a referral interview with someone in a position to offer you a job. If this doesn't happen, then ask for some referrals. Listen to all the advice. Revise your résumé after every interview. And keep polishing it. And keep an open mind, like one young applicant who went for a job in a radio

124

George Harrison
1943–2001

CLASS 95 FM

RADIO STATION CLASS 95 FM MARKED THE DEATH OF GEORGE HARRISON WITH THIS SIMPLE, APPROPRIATE VISUAL CREATED BY DENTSU YOUNG & RUBICAM SINGAPORE.

station. The station manager had nothing to offer, but on the basis of the applicant's writing ability sent him to the owner of an ad agency who hired him on the spot.

It may sound insidious, but many jobs do come through contacts and networking. No matter how good you are, no one will know of you if they have not heard of you.

Send in your résumé to the top of the hiring chain to maximise readership. As your application moves down the hierarchy, it may just spark interest. Make the layout and presentation of your résumé creative. Even gimmicks have been known to work as a last resort. In fact copywriters usually come up with the most creative approaches to finding a job. For example, a copywriter sent a completely realistic milk carton with his picture and the words, "Have you seen this man?", on the side. A phone number was included for prospective employers to call. One young Australian posed as a court official, arrived at agencies with a summons for the creative director, and all doors opened. Another real-life example was Kimberly Kasitz, a fresh graduate who knew her lack of experience would be a stumbling block. So she wrote her résumé in the form of a newspaper article. She not only got a job, but also established an entire network because of this ingenious act.

But gimmicks can only take you so far. Substance is what matters during the interview. Once you get an appointment, you will need to start preparing. Think of the questions you'll most likely be asked. For sure one of them will be: "Why do you want to work in advertising?" Answers like, "It's cool" or "All advertising people drive Porsches" won't get you far. Run through an imaginary interview in your head, and practise what you want to say out loud to a friend. This may be harder than you think, because it usually isn't in character to brag about one's abilities unless you're an egomaniac.

You'll also need to figure out what to wear. If you have really bad fashion sense, or if you're just not sure, take a walk down to the company to see what their employees wear. Following what they wear might even give the interviewer the impression that you'll be able to fit right in. Always remember to dress in a way that fits the job description. If the job requires a lot of travelling, dress ruggedly to show your willingness to hit the road. If you can, get a portfolio case to store your spec work and a briefcase for everything else. You may want to include any pieces of good writing that you have done — if you're a graduate that doesn't mean people automatically believe you can write well.

You're now at the interview site. First, go to the restroom because you may not see one again for a while. Then, observe your environment and chat with the people working there. Make friends with the receptionist and secretaries; remember that you need a network. This is also your chance to feel out the company and soak up the atmosphere; then you can tactfully ask the interviewer questions on things you are ambivalent about. You must always make sure that your commitment to work in the company is rock hard, so clarify all points of doubt. During the interview proper, interviewers sometimes ask you to talk about your work. If they don't, find an opportunity to bring it up. Be sincere and passionate, but don't appear too egotistical. Sit at the edge of your chair to show enthusiasm; if you sit back completely you'll look too relaxed, too easy-going. Although taking notes turns off some interviewers, do keep writing materials handy. This is especially important if you have many interviews and want to remember who said what.

In general, you should answer all of the interviewer's questions by considering the strengths that you want to highlight in the interview. Try and show how these strengths can help the company solve its problems. When the questions become somewhat acidic, rephrase them in a positive light. Example:

INTERVIEWER: WHAT? YOU STUDIED GEOLOGY? WHAT GOOD IS THAT?

YOU: MY STUDYING GEOLOGY CAN HELP YOUR COMPANY AS THE ANALYTICAL SKILLS I LEARNT ALLOW ME TO BE MORE OBJECTIVE AND SENSITIVE TO THE MANY VIEWPOINTS IN ANY SITUATION. FOR INSTANCE, IT'S HELPED ME DEVELOP A KNACK FOR DETAILS THAT WOULD BE USEFUL IN RECALLING FACTS AND FIGURES.

The interviewer might also ask you to discuss your weaknesses. One way to deflect attention from the shortcomings is to emphasize your strengths. Example:

INTERVIEWER: YOU ONLY GOT A "C" FOR HISTORY. WHY?
YOU: HISTORY IS A SUBJECT THAT REQUIRES A LOT OF MEMORISING. I'M NOT GOOD AT THAT, BUT I'M A QUICK THINKER, WHICH MAY BE A SKILL SUITED TO YOUR COMPANY'S NEEDS.

Admitting to a weakness may backfire, but it may also earn you points for honesty. Example:

INTERVIEWER: NAME ONE OF YOUR WEAKNESSES.
YOU: I'M VERY SHY AND HAVE SOME DIFFICULTY COMMUNICATING WITH OTHERS AT FIRST, BUT I CAN BE VERY FRIENDLY ONCE I WARM UP TO PEOPLE.

Always conclude the interview on a positive note. As with writing, people pay attention at the start and at the end of the interview, so if you have a bad ending try to correct it before you leave the room. Ask for comments from your interviewer — what they liked about you, how you could improve your career prospects. If your enthusiasm has shone through, people will be more than willing to give you constructive comments. However, don't change your interview style at every new suggestion. Different people have different likes, so compile advice from at least three interviews before you make any changes. Finally, ask for the interviewer's business card and leave a copy of your résumé and any sample pieces behind. Then they can look at your samples and be able to link them to you.

After the interview, you're not done yet. Send a thank-you note to your interviewer. That is why you asked for a business card. Not many people take the time to show their gratitude, so those who do will stand out. Make sure you watch your grammar and spelling here as well. Specify some point in the interview that you wish to clarify or comment on — this shows you were paying attention. In fact, it will be even better if you can send a copy of a revised résumé incorporating their suggestions for improvement and ask for a second interview by showing interest in hearing more feedback. Even if you get notice that you've been dropped, continue calling the company to show that you still have interest in working there. Importantly, never leave an interview without gaining something from it, whether it's advice or another referral. Remember that getting a job in the competitive field of advertising is a drawn-out process, and only those who persevere will succeed.

WHAT A CREATIVE DIRECTOR SAYS...

Award-winning writer Paul Fishlock at Sydney's Brown Melhuish Fishlock has this advice: "I ask young, untrained, fresh-out-of-school wannabes to tell me about three things he or she has bought in the last week and why they were chosen over other options. Why? Because you can't hope to understand and influence other people's buying behaviour if you don't understand your own. If they're honest, their answers are more likely to be 'because it was cheaper', or 'it came with 25% free', or 'it was the only one in the shop', or 'my friend's got one', rather than 'I chose it because the ad made me laugh'."

"I AM OFTEN ASKED HOW I GOT INTO THIS BUSINESS. I DIDN'T. THE BUSINESS GOT INTO ME." LEO BURNETT

HOW TO HANDLE
REJECTIONS

The important thing to understand here is that if the human resource department rejects you, they may tell you that you will be considered for future positions. However, now that your résumé is together with thousands of other rejected résumés, the chances of that happening are close to zero. The key strategy here is to correspond directly with the manager who has put out the hiring request. Of course, you will need to do some research on this, and a network of contacts in the industry will be of great help. This way, you not only bypass the HR people, you may also impress the manager with your determination.

HOW TO PROVE YOU'RE CREATIVE
WHEN YOU'VE DONE NOTHING CREATIVE

If you want to enter the creative field, you will only succeed when you have passion — *sincere passion*. Once you have decided this is truly your line of work, you should learn about the advertising companies that you wish to work for, and if possible their clients. Opportunities also await you in places other than agencies, such as government agencies or department stores that have in-house advertising sections.

Would-be young copywriters and art directors should never go empty-handed to an interview. The most important part of the interview will be your portfolio. Agency creative directors are looking for raw talent with maximum potential. If they are going to invest time and effort training you, they want some idea of your talent first. The best way to show you're passionate and talented is to take ads from the newspaper, study them, understand what they are trying to communicate, then rewrite them in your own words, and lay them out in your own style. The CDs won't expect highly polished professional standards, but it will give them an idea of how you think creatively.

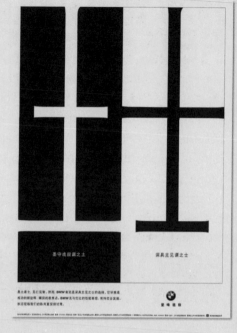

MANY ASIAN CAMPA
IN TWO DIFFERENT LA
CAMPAIGN FROM M&
WAS FIRST CONCEIV
TRANSLATED INTO EI

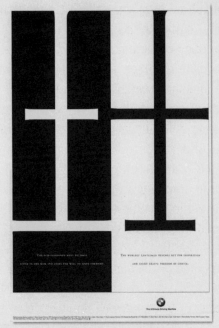

GNS HAVE TO WORK
NGUAGES. THIS BMW
SAATCHI SINGAPORE
IN CHINESE AND
GLISH.

Show how you can come up with creative solutions for the agency by doing some spec ideas for its clients. (This is where your research of the company comes in handy.) You're likely to attract more attention as well as stimulate a longer, more productive interview — but mind you don't criticise the agency's work! Alternatively, pick a product that isn't widely advertised (like green beans) so that your work will stand out from the clutter. Try to avoid products that usually have standard themes, unless you've found a truly new way of doing it.

If you can, come up with pieces for a campaign — the ability to keep a theme constant throughout a series of ads without forsaking the distinction between each one will truly showcase your capabilities. The execution of your specs must show your understanding of budget constraints, so keep your ideas practical. What you have in your portfolio will be deemed as your best work, and a reflection of your creative attitude.

Young art directors can also show their college work, but remove all the mediocre pieces even if they are your favourites. Don't keep any slipshod work inside. If you have to redo an entire piece because of one spaghetti stain, just redo it. Your specs must show your understanding of the advantages and disadvantages of various techniques such as photography or watercolours, and the different production limitations of newspapers and magazines. (Like remembering to allow space for the gutter when running headlines across two facing pages in a magazine!) Variety in your selection is important.

Just before the interview, run through your portfolio mentally. You're going to have to explain your work, and you won't want to stumble in the process. At the same time, you've got to make sure that the pieces can speak for themselves because you may have to leave them with the interviewer.

Whatever you do, don't just go in with lots of "clever" ads for condoms. Do ads for real accounts like cars, cosmetics, appliances and retailers. And never copy ads you've seen in award books — you'll be caught immediately!

MAKE YOUR OWN ADS
AND MAKE AN IMPRESSION

Frank Todaro, @radical.media New York, was ranked the world's third most-awarded TV commercial director in 2000. His advice: "You can shoot an ad and edit it on your laptop. The software is there. If you think you would really like to do it, then just try to do it. Even if it's not broadcast quality, you can show what it is you can do."

STARTING SALARIES:
WHAT YOU CAN EXPECT
IN YEAR ONE

AUSTRALIA From Gerri Dibsdall of Dibsdall Weekes and Mary Garcia-Martinez of MGM in Sydney:
- Junior A/E: A$30,000–35,000 per year
- Junior planner: A$45,000 per year
- Media assistant: A$35,000–40,000 per year
- Junior copywriter: A$25,000 per year*
- Junior art director: A$25,000 per year*

(*Starting salaries applicable to AWARD School graduates or those having six months' experience)

HONG KONG From Michele Crew of The Crew Partnership Ltd:
- Junior A/E: Ranging from HK$91,000–130,000 per year
- Junior planner: HK$117,000–130,000 per year
- Media assistant: HK$91,000–117,000 per year
- Junior copywriter: HK$78,000–91,000 per year
- Junior art director: HK$78,000–91,000 per year

(Salaries at junior level include Chinese New Year extra month bonus.)

MALAYSIA Eddy Chin, executive director of the Association of Accredited Advertising Agents Malaysia advises that the average annual starting pay at agencies is RM18,000 per year for degree holders and RM7,200 per year for diploma holders, irrespective of whether you are in account service, media or creative. Some smaller agencies pay better start-up salaries than multinationals because they hire people to perform multiple roles — for example, junior A/Es who are first jobholders will also plan and buy media. There is a perceived value in 2 + 1 and 3 + 0 tertiary education programmes in Malaysia via twinning with Australian universities like Monash, Curtin and Deakin, or with universities in the UK and US. Candidates with degrees earned entirely overseas may have a slight edge over a local grad or one who has done a twinning programme. Candidates with experience and known performance will always have an advantage. A serious shortage in servicing, creative or media personnel will force salaries upward. Chin also believes agencies are realising the availability of skills outside their current pool of candidates; people from marketing, banking, catering, sales, promotions, even law, can bring new efficiencies to agencies and enhance their service to clients.

SINGAPORE Based on starting salary data supplied by 10AM Communications, M&C Saatchi, AdGrand Advertising, Crush Advertising, Henen Advertising, and Saatchi & Saatchi:

- Junior A/E: S$20,000–30,000 per year
- Junior planner: S$20,000–36,000 per year
- Media assistant: S$18,000–30,000 per year
- Junior copywriter: S$20,000–42,000 per year
- Junior art director: S$20,000–42,000 per year

THAILAND From Dan Sornmani, managing director of Batey Ads Thailand:
- Junior A/E: 120,000–300,000 baht per year
- Media assistant: From 144,000 baht per year
- Junior copywriter: 180,000–360,000 baht per year
- Junior art director: 180,000–360,000 baht per year

UK From London's Joyce McMillan:
- A/E (graduate): From £25,000 per year
- Junior planner (graduate): £25,000–35,000 per year. And the sky's the limit for really good senior planners.
- Media assistant: £18,000–20,000 per year. After two years' experience, salaries of £35,000 upwards are not unusual.
- Junior copywriter: On a permanent basis from about £20,000 per year, depending on the agency.
- Junior art director: On a permanent basis from about £20,000 per year, depending on the agency.

US From Nancy Temkin of Greenberg Kirshenbaum:
- A/E: US$30,000–35,000 per year
- Planner: Generally no entry level positions. With experience, US$55,000–65,000 per year
- Media assistant: US$25,000–30,000 per year
- Junior copywriter: US$30,000–40,000
- Junior art director: US$30,000–40,000

Totally devoted

FOOTBALL CHANNEL

**ADVERTISING SHOULD ALW
NEEDS. DENTSU YOUNG &
DEVELOPED THIS CAMPAI
VISION'S FOOTBALL CHA
VIEWERS WHO WERE DE**

Totally devoted

FOOTBALL CHANNEL

YS ANSWER CONSUMER
UBICAM SINGAPORE
FOR SINGAPORE CABLE
EL AND TARGETED
ED TO FOOTBALL.

HOW MUCH MONEY
ARE YOU WORTH?

The top creative people everywhere will tell you to sacrifice everything to work in a great creative agency. If you work in a bad agency, your talent won't develop; even worse, it will become stunted and your career could be set back by years.

Because most advertising skills are learned on the job, great young creative stars come from working in creative environments where they learn from great writers and art directors. President and creative director of Fallon Minneapolis David Lubars explains the critical choice young creatives have to make: "If you go for the money early, you're hurting yourself in the long term. The best places are either big — so they can afford NOT to give you so much money because everyone wants to go there — or they're small and they can't afford to give you that money. If you want to go into creative and have a long-term career, it's not about the money when you begin. In your 20s, don't think about money. The thing is, when you don't think about the money and you get the work, the money comes; much more money than you could have made working your way up in some middle-level company that's mediocre. The money comes from fame and success in the marketplace, so you have to be in a place where you can have that."

HOW CAN HEADHUNTERS HELP?

Other than conducting your own job campaign through human resource (HR) departments, you can also seek job placement help through two other avenues: employment agencies and headhunters (or executive search firms). It is easy to confuse these two, especially since there has been a blurring of their roles. Still, there are strategies and precautions to take between the two, and the point is to utilise all of these means of employment and not throw your whole lot in with just one of them. So, let's find out more about these channels.

While the HR department is within the ad agency's jurisdiction, employment agencies and headhunters work independently. **Job placement agencies** generally cater to more junior positions. One of the reasons is that they only get paid when someone is successfully hired, so it helps when the applicant's asking price is low. Traditionally known as flesh peddlers because of their indiscriminate placement habits, most agencies will now conduct interviews to screen applicants first. Payments also come in many ways. The applicant may be asked to foot the entire placement fee, or the employer may decide to take the entire cost. The payment division can sometimes be negotiated between the employer and the applicant, with the portion paid by the applicant reimbursed over time. On the other hand, the fee can also resemble a loan taken out by the applicant, with the company footing the cost upfront and collecting it back from the applicant's salary.

When you seek help at an employment agency, you're basically counting on fate to get a job. In a mainstream industry, just multiply 500 résumés by the number of agencies with the same listing and you can see the numbers you're up against. So, what can you do to increase your chances? Firstly, make sure your agency is full of hustle and bustle. The more traffic there is the higher your chances of getting a placement. Try to schedule an appointment with the placement manager if possible, since this will give a face to the hundreds of résumés they receive. While you're at it, find out what you can about the agency. Some agencies may have a special contract with a specific company, or concentrate on employment opportunities in a specific industry. This is important because a wide spread for your résumé may be good, but it may also be detrimental because it decreases your market value. When a company receives three copies of your résumé, they'll probably drop you. Once you're with an agency, always keep in touch so that you aren't just part of the multitude of résumés. A call once every two weeks will keep you in the placement manager's mind when a new offer comes up.

Executive search firms, on the other hand, deal with the placement of senior executives. They don't keep a file of "applicants", but a list of "candidates". They are called "headhunters" because of their aggressive networking. This is crucial because headhunters are more interested in getting people who are already hired. They are not there for the job hunters, but work instead for the potential employer, and there is usually a close working relationship between the two. These days, many agencies have no time to see new talent. They only hire through headhunters, trusting the headhunters to filter out the less talented candidates.

Headhunters consider a candidate's willingness to accept a job as an important factor since they only get paid when the deal goes through. Some headhunters, however, get paid a retainer (about 33% of an executive's first-year salary) whether or not they find a successful candidate. Therefore, a candidate's marketability and credentials are of utmost importance to them. They are also obliged to conduct more thorough screenings of their candidates than a placement agency. Most executive search firms even offer their clients a money back guarantee if the candidate is rejected or resigns within a certain period after being hired.

The system works two ways. Once copywriters and art directors have some great ads in their books and some great awards behind them, or when young account service executives have a strong track on some major accounts, they're ready to talk to a headhunter. You can call up for an interview, and provided that they like your talent and personality you will be "on their books". When one of their clients asks them to find someone like you, you'll be sent for a job interview.

If you have built a well-known reputation in the industry, and your name has appeared often in the trade press, the headhunter might call you at work out of the blue and persuade you to meet with their client. (This often happens in advertising because some ad agencies are reluctant to poach staff directly from their competitors; they prefer the headhunter to make the initial overture.)

Either way, headhunters are paid by the employers, not by you. A responsible headhunter is rather like an agent, bringing together employees and employers. They will advise candidates which job offers to pursue and which may not be quite suited to their personalities. They will also be objective with agencies and only put forward the right candidates; some headhunters have hundreds of names on their books, but only a handful might be selected for a particular vacancy.

It may sound very mercenary, but that's not always the case. Many headhunters are passionate advocates of industry training schemes. Some headhunters go out of their way, and sacrifice fees, in order to help young people with genuine talent to get started. Ask around in the industry; you'll soon find out which headhunters have developed lasting relationships with young talent.

WHAT SHOULD YOU DO WHEN A HEADHUNTER CALLS?

The call can come when you least expect it, and it will be much better to reschedule the call so that you can take it at home. After all, if your boss finds out that you're looking around for a new job, you'll probably be passed over for promotions and other opportunities.

Rescheduling the call will also give you time to check up on the background of the firm and if it is well established. Sometimes the headhunter is simply asking for a referral, so do a good deed and recommend a friend. This friend will probably return the favour in the future, and the headhunter could also be indirectly learning more about you.

In any event, never reveal information about anything until you can confirm that there is a job vacancy. This is especially true when it concerns your salary. Headhunters will usually up your asking price by 10 to 20%, so if you're underpaid, give them an asking price instead. Don't tell lies though — if the firm is a bona fide one, they'll find out the truth about you sooner or later.

Another thing you shouldn't reveal is that you may be working with other headhunters. Unscrupulous headhunters may use your information to find new business, or drop you entirely since there is less chance of placing you. At the same time, be honest if you aren't interested in the job they are offering. Advertising is a small world and you should gain a reputation for being frank. Some candidates waste everybody's time and you won't be thanked for that!

Since the headhunter could simply be testing the ground, the only way for you to impress is through your conversation. If you sound like headhunters always call you anyway, it will just elevate your status all that much higher. Finally, give an impression that all is well in your job, and that you may not be looking, but will consider good offers that come by. The latter point is crucial. You want to play hard to get, but at the same time you don't want to close the door on a better job by playing too hard.

Ultimately, headhunters will become your allies if you end up on the shortlist since their close contact with the potential employer will allow them to give you advice as well.

THIS DEMONSTRATION OF STRENGTH FOR SAMSONITE WAS CREATED BY TBWA SINGAPORE. THE VISUAL METAPHOR WAS A BRIEF CASE MORE IMPACT RESISTANT THAN AN AIRCRAFT FLIGHT RECORDER.

WHAT A HEADHUNTER SAYS...

Michele Crew at Hong Kong's The Crew Partnership Ltd says: "Creative always remains a key opportunity. There are huge differences in salaries. The biggest and most ugly accounts, where opportunities to learn your craft creatively would be severely skewed, pay highly. The best creative shops pay abysmally, but are worth every lost penny in terms of creative development and future big bucks. Account service is less volatile, but increasingly not what the industry needs. There are virtually no junior planners with a year's experience; planning is a key opportunity for growth and would make good career advice for undergraduates.

"Although creatives come out of this less well within year one, it's worth noting that in years two and three junior creatives may find themselves increasing their salaries at least 10% quicker than media and account service peers. By the time people in advertising have hit the five-year mark, they are generally paid as much as 35% more than their peers in other service industries."

THESE BOOKS MAY HELP...

· **AITCHISON, JIM (1999)**
Cutting Edge Advertising, Singapore: Prentice Hall.
· **AITCHISON, JIM (2001)**
Cutting Edge Commercial, Singapore: Prentice Hall.
· **BARRY, ANN MARIE (1990)**
The Advertising Portfolio: Creating an Effective Presentation of Your Work, Lincolnwood, Ill., USA: NTC Business Books.

· **COHEN, WILLIAM A. (1978)**
"How to Get a Job Through a Corporate Headhunter," in *The Executive's Guide to Finding a Superior Job*, New York, NY: AMACOM, 86–94.

· **DEVRIES, HENRY AND DIANE GAGE (1991)**
The Self-Marketing Secret: Winning by Making Your Name Known, San Marcos, CA: Avant Books.

· **HAMEROFF, EUGENE J. (1998)**
The Advertising Agency Business: The Complete Manual for Management & Operation, 3rd ed., Lincolnwood, IL.: NTC Business Books.

· **HASHIM, ADNAN (1994)**
Advertising in Malaysia, Pelanduk Publications Malaysia.

· **JONES, STEPHANIE (1995)**
"Careers and Executive Search," in *Headhunting: A Guide to Executive Search in Asia*, Singapore: Prentice Hall, 171–190.

· **LOCKER, KITTY O. (1992)**
Business and Administrative Communication, 2nd ed., Homewood, IL.: Irwin.

· **OGILVY, DAVID (1964)**
Confessions of an Advertising Man, New York: Longman.

· **ROMAN, KEN AND JEAN MASS (1976)**
How to Advertise, New York: St Martin's Press.

· **SALZ, NANCY L. (1994)**
How to Get the Best Advertising from Your Agency: The Guide to Quickly Building a Productive Team, 3rd ed., Burr Ridge, IL.: Irwin Professional.

· **WEINSTEIN, BOB (1997)**
"The Truth About Human Resource Folks, Placement Managers, and Headhunters," in *Who Says There Are No Jobs Out There? 25 Irreverent Rules for Getting a Job*, New York, NY: McGraw-Hill, 115–125.

ONCE YOU'VE GOT THE JOB, HOW SHOULD YOU BUILD YOUR CAREER?

Someone once said advertising is a marathon not a race. Singapore's Linda Locke started as an art director at Batey Ads, switching to Leo Burnett where she was the only woman in an all-male department. At Saatchi & Saatchi she rose to the position of creative director and later CEO, eventually returning to Leo Burnett as regional creative director and chairman — all within 20 years.

Sometimes young people put too much pressure on themselves and risk early burnout. "Advertising is not a cure for cancer," says Scott Whybin of Melbourne's Whybin TBWA & Partners. "It's not that serious. It's not going to change the world. You can have passion and ambition, and all those things, but at the end of the day you've got to have a deliberate detachment from it. The people who get it all wrong are the ones who get so worked up about it. If you're obsessed with awards, if you start thinking, oh, this one will be a short walk (to the stage), you'll always be B-grade."

David Blackley, chairman of Clemenger BBDO Melbourne, talks about the burnout spiral traps young creatives fall into. "They change agencies every 18 months and get quite a bit of publicity for it, but they spin out of the business relatively early. They're in it for some sort of ego reasons or they're so into advertising that they only mix with advertising people; they only go to advertising pubs, they only go to advertising club lunches, they only go to advertising parties on the weekends. They're so caught up in the peer group thing they lose reality for the things outside. I love good advertising with a passion, but I think you can only do it with a wider perspective. *You've got to experience what real people experience.* It's a bit like the old barrel; if you've got the tap on, pouring the ideas out at the bottom, you've got to keep putting a wide variety of stuff in at the top."

TO SURVIVE ALL THE CRISES AND REJECTIONS, THE BEST TALENT DEVELOPS RESILIENCE AND KNOWS HOW TO HIT PEAK PERFORMANCE LEVELS WITHOUT TOO MUCH STRESS. THEY ALSO HAVE A POSITIVE OUTLOOK LIKE AMERICAN ADVERTISING GURU HAL RINEY. RINEY SAYS ADVERTISING PEOPLE ARE LUCKY, BECAUSE "WE HAVE A NEW LIFE EVERY DAY IN ADVERTISING."

Young creatives face special pressures. At Lowe Lintas & Partners US, Gary Goldsmith believes the best creative people have their own personal creative processes and says these processes can be improved. "After an assignment is over, stop and think about it. What happened when you did good ads? What did you do *differently* than the times when you did bad ads? Then think about how you've got to do those things more often than not, like an athlete. If great athletes could only perform occasionally, it'd be terrible." Goldsmith's advice for young creatives is to be patient *and* impatient at the same time. "Always be fighting to try to do more work, good work, but cut yourself a break. Don't expect that you're going to get out and be the world's best writer or art director in the first year. Give yourself a chance. Be resilient. People get too discouraged way too early now. Just go in every day and try to do something good."

But once you do achieve success, in account service, creative or media, watch for the danger signs like apathy and being overly confident. Steve Henry warns that creative people particularly should never feel self-satisfied. Multi-award winning Singaporean Kash Sree, now at Wieden & Kennedy Portland, agrees. He deftly dismisses his own achievements. "I haven't done anything yet. I haven't done anything that is so different or so great that I can sit back and think, I can't do better than that. The best advertising comes from really insecure people, people who are never satisfied. Always be hungry, always work harder than the next guy, always question everything — especially yourself."

THINKING OUTSIDE THE BOX: BBDO BANGKOK PUT A RIVAL COURIER'S BOX INSIDE A FEDERAL EXPRESS BOX TO SUGGEST WHICH COURIER SERVICE WAS FASTER.

TIPS
FROM THE TOP

When you first join the business, Mike Cozens has this advice: "Concentrate on doing things other people don't want to do. Become a great radio writer because no one else is."

Siimon Reynolds was Australia's most famous creative director when he was only 22. He knew people were waiting for him to fail. One of his secrets was *creative quarantine*. "The average person's brain is 90% full of bad, ordinary ads because that's what you see all around you. But what we used to do was never read a newspaper and never watch TV. If we saw ads, they were only the world's best. We watched the world's best TV commercials on reels. If we saw print ads, they were only the world's best print ads in annuals. So after a few years all your brain had in it, as a point of reference, were great ads. Immediately you sat down to do an ad, you worked to a different yardstick..." Reynolds says you must become a great creative in your mind before the reality can happen. "Firstly, learn the structures of great work; secondly, learn to reject a lot of your own work; thirdly, you must really want success. It can't be a casual ambition..."

MAY LWIN

MAY LWIN (PH.D.) IS AN ASSISTANT PROFESSOR IN THE DEPARTMENT OF MARKETING, AT THE NATIONAL UNIVERSITY OF SINGAPORE. HAVING PREVIOUSLY WORKED AT CITIBANK N.A. AND WITH OGILVY & MATHER ADVERTISING, HER TEACHING SUBJECTS AT THE NUS BUSINESS SCHOOL INCLUDE PROMOTIONS AND RETAIL MANAGEMENT. HER RESEARCH HAS DEALT WITH ADVERTISING REGULATIONS AND ETHICS AS WELL AS ADVERTISING IN CROSS-CULTURAL CONTEXTS. SHE HAS PUBLISHED IN A NUMBER OF INTERNATIONAL AND REGIONAL JOURNALS, HAS CO-AUTHORED A BOOK ON MARKETING CASES IN ASIA, AND CONTRIBUTED TO OTHER MAJOR MARKETING TEXTS.

JIM AITCHISON

JIM AITCHISON, AN AUSTRALIAN, WAS FORMER CREATIVE DIRECTOR OF THE LEGENDARY BALL PARTNERSHIP AND BATEY ADS, SINGAPORE. HE HAS WON HUNDREDS OF AWARDS. HE HAS JUDGED MANY MAJOR AWARD SHOWS AND SPOKEN AT SEMINARS AND CREATIVE WORKSHOPS IN AUSTRALIA, CANADA, MALAYSIA, THAILAND AND THE US. AFTER 20 YEARS IN ADVERTISING, HE IS NOW AN AUTHOR, ACTOR AND RADIO HOST. HIS BOOKS, CUTTING EDGE ADVERTISING AND CUTTING EDGE COMMERCIALS (BOTH PUBLISHED BY PEARSON EDUCATION), HAVE BECOME BEST SELLERS AROUND THE WORLD. JIM'S VOICE CAN BE HEARD IN HUNDREDS OF TELEVISION AND RADIO COMMERCIALS.

ACKNOWLEDGEMENTS

THE AUTHORS WOULD LIKE TO THANK EVERYONE WHO CONTRIBUTED THEIR TIME AND WISDOM TO THE WRITING OF THIS BOOK, INCLUDING JOSEPH TAN WHO HELPED WITH THE RESEARCH. THANKS TO THE GREAT ADVERTISING AGENCIES WHO GAVE THEIR PERMISSION FOR THEIR WORK TO APPEAR IN THIS BOOK. WE'D LIKE TO THANK THESEUS CHAN AT WORK SINGAPORE FOR DESIGNING OUR BOOK, AND ANDIE NGOH AND EVONNE NG FOR ALL THEIR HARD WORK. OUR THANKS TO JOHNSON TAN AND HIS TEAM AT PROCOLOR SINGAPORE FOR THEIR SPECIAL HELP, TOO. THANKS, TOO, TO THE MUSEUM OF THE CITY OF NEW YORK FOR PERMISSION TO REPRODUCE PHOTOGRAPHS OF EARLY AMERICAN ADVERTISING FROM THE BYRON COLLECTION.